# RUNNING WORKSHOPS

# RUNNING WORKSHOPS

A Guide for Trainers in the Helping Professions

## THE OPEN UNIVERSITY COPING WITH CRISIS RESEARCH GROUP

CROOM HELM
London • Sydney • Wolfeboro, New Hampshire

© 1987 The Coping with Crisis Research and Training Group,
Open University
Croom Helm Ltd, Provident House, Burrell Row,
Beckenham, Kent BR3 1AT
Croom Helm Australia, 44-50 Waterloo Road,
North Ryde, 2113, New South Wales

British Library Cataloguing in Publication Data

Running workshops: a guide for trainers
in the helping professions.
1. Social word education — Great Britain
I. Open University. *Coping with Crisis
Research and Training Group*
361'.007'041   HV11
ISBN 0-7099-4809-3


Croom Helm, 27 South Main Street, Wolfeboro,
New Hampshire 03894-2069

**Library of Congress Cataloging-in-Publication Data**

Running workshops.

    1. Social workers — In-service training. I. Open
University. Coping with Crisis Research and Training
Group.
HV40.5.R86  1987      361.3'07'15      86-24372
ISBN 0-7099-4809-3


Printed and bound in Great Britain by
Biddles Ltd, Guildford and King's Lynn

CONTENTS

Preface

MEMBERS OF "COPING WITH CRISIS RESEARCH GROUP" : SOME
BIOGRAPHICAL DETAILS

Chris Bundy completed training as a State Registered Nurse in
1978, and as a Registered Mental Nurse in 1980. She graduated
with an honours degree in Applied Psychology from the
University of Wales, Institute of Science and Technology in
1984.
She has worked as a tutor on the government sponsored
Youth Training Scheme, running workshops using both experiential learning and small group techniques. She has been employed
as a research psychologist in the Family Institute in Cardiff,
and in the South Birmingham District Psychology Service.

Tony Hobbs is a senior clinical psychologist working in adult
mental health and is based at Whitchurch Hospital, Cardiff,
Wales. Having graduated in Psychology from Leeds University in
1975, he took the one year post-graduate diploma in Counselling
in Educational Settings at Aston University. In the intervening
years before undertaking clinical training, he worked as a
counsellor/administrator with the British Pregnancy Advisory
Service, as warden of St. Mary's Tyndalls Park Trust, Bristol
(a residential treatment centre for emotionally disturbed
adolescents), and as student counsellor at North East London
Polytechnic.

Camilla Lambert has been a member of the Coping With Crisis
Research Group since its start and has worked as an Open
University tutor-counsellor for the last nine years. Her
employment experience is largely in research and adult education, most recently in evaluating the Open University version
of the Certificate in Health Education. She is now moving into
Health Education, working on the prevention of drug misuse as
a Health Education Officer in Gwent.

Stephen Murgatroyd worked for the Open University between 1975
and 1985 as a researcher and senior counsellor. Co-founder of
the Coping With Crisis Research Group, Stephen is now
Professor of Applied Psychology and Dean of Administrative

Members of "Coping With Crisis Research Group" : Some
Biographical Details

Studies at Athabasca University in Alberta, Canada. Formerly
Editor of The Counsellor and Assistant Editor of The British
Journal of Guidance and Counselling, Stephen has made a major
contribution to counselling psychology in Britain. He has
authored or co-authored Helping the Troubled Child, Coping With
Crisis (with Ray Woolfe), Helping Families in Distress (with
Ray Woolfe) and Counselling and Helping. He is a fellow of the
British Psychological Society.

Dick Pates is a clinical psychologist working in Cardiff.
Following a first degree in Applied Social Psychology at the
University of Wales Institute of Science and Technology, he
did a clinical training at the Welsh In-service Training Centre.
    He formerly worked with children and adolescents and with
sexual and marital therapy with couples in Cardiff. He is now
employed as Senior Clinical Psychologist on the community
drugs team in Cardiff.
    He has run workshops on sexuality for several years in
Wales with a wide variety of groups.

Sylvia Rhys is a tutor and counsellor with the Open University
in Wales. She has worked as a researcher for the Institute of
Health Care Studies at University College, Swansea and for the
extra-mural department at the University College, Cardiff. She
is co-author with Stephen Murgatroyd and Ray Woolfe of a book
(in print) on Guidance and Counselling in Adult and Continuing
Education.

Dr. Michael Shooter is a consultant in Child, Adolescent and
Family Psychiatry, working as part of a multidisciplinary,
non-hierarchical, non-medically orientated team at Preswylfa
Child and Family Centre, Cardiff.
    The team believes in helping people with problems as they
see them and in the context in which they live. It aims to
have sufficient range of skills to tailor help to the clients
rather than the other way round!

Ray Woolfe, co-founder of the Coping With Crisis Research
Group, has worked for the past thirteen years as a Senior
Lecturer in Education (Staff Tutor) for the Open University,
first in Cardiff and then in Manchester. He is a member of the
National Executives of respectively the Counselling Section of
the British Psychological Society and the British Association
for Counselling and chairs the B.A.C.s Publications Group. He
is the author of two major books on counselling; Coping With
Crisis (with Stephen Murgatroyd), and Helping Families in
Distress (with Stephen Murgatroyd), and has wide experience of
running workshops both in Britain and abroad. He is aged 44,
is a practising marriage guidance counsellor and is married
with two children.

PREFACE

The Coping With Crisis Research Group within the Open
University is a co-operative group. It aims to develop an
understanding of the ways in which adults and young people
cope with stressful life events. Founded in 1979 by Stephen
Murgatroyd and Ray Woolfe, it has as its members full and
part-time members of the staff of the Open University and
colleagues from social work, psychiatry and clinical psychology.
     Between 1980 and 1984 the group ran a number of workshops
aimed at developing coping and helping skills through structured experiences, reflection, teaching and personally significant learning. This book documents this experience.
     The book aims to present the details of workshops on
stress, death, sexuality, helping and basic counselling and
communication skills. Each chapter is written by the workshop
organiser and describes how the workshop was organised and
executed and why. In addition, some broad issues of principle
concerning experiential learning and evaluation are examined
in introductory and concluding chapters.
     The book has been written using the group as a basis for
detailed discussion of each chapter. Ray Woolfe and Stephen
Murgatroyd acted as leading organisers of this project. The
opinions expressed in each chapter are those of the individual
contributor. The preparation of the manuscript was undertaken
by Christine Horner, to whom the editors are indebted.
     You can find out more about the Coping With Crisis
Research Group from Ray Woolfe, The Open University, North
West Regional Centre, Chorlton House, 70 Manchester Road,
Chorlton-cum-Hardy, Manchester M21 1PQ.

Chapter One

EXPERIENTIAL LEARNING IN WORKSHOPS

RAY WOOLFE

INTRODUCTION

This book does not purport to be a complete manual to workshop
practice. For a start its selection of topics is partial,
though wide in scope. Each chapter consists of an account of a
workshop on a particular theme and most chapters are detailed
enough for the reader to construct his or her own workshop
from the framework provided. However, we do not pretend that
each framework is the only possible one in that particular
field. Nevertheless, while this may not be an encyclopaedic
manual, we see it as a guide to workshop practice and the book
contains an additional ingredient not usually found in manuals:
each chapter aims to give not just a description of what happened, but also to describe what it felt like. In other words we
are concerned with offering you a flavour of each workshop
over and above the bare bones of describing its objectives,
methodology, structure and operation. The book contains no
hard data though we are very much concerned with the issue of
evaluation and we do provide a substantial final chapter on
this very subject.
     The book contains eight chapters by six writers; two
chapters each by Woolfe and Murgatroyd and one each from Hobbs,
Pates, Rhys and Shooter. Inevitably the number of writers and
the fact that they come from a variety of backgrounds with
different experiences means that there are subtle differences
in emphasis, orientation and interpretation as well as differences in the use of language. Thus terms like trainer, facilitator, leader and organiser are used in specific ways by
specific writers as they see appropriate. We did not see the
need to edit out such differences. They give the book its
character and emphasise, if emphasis is needed, that though
groups may possess their own characteristics, in the end they
consist of a number of individuals who come together to achieve
a common purpose. Therefore, we accept, indeed point to individual differences while at the same time stressing the collec-
tive nature of the product and the things in common which

brought this group of people together and the experiences they
have shared. This book is an attempt to share these experiences
with a wider audience. Its philosophy derives from the commitment of its members to client centred helping and student
centred learning, yet encompassed within a framework which we
regard as pragmatic. We use this term as meaning a commitment
to employ any technique, humanistic, psychodynamic or behavior-
ist, where this can be agreed between trainer and student as
being potentially helpful to the latter's learning. Our experience suggests that the term which overall best describes our
educational methodology is that of 'experiential learning' and
the subject of experiential learning offers the framework for
this first chapter, which attempts to define and explore the
meaning of the term. In doing this the chapter will provide
some kind of introduction to what is to come in the rest of
the book, to give some idea of content, themes and the general
approach which is to follow.

The field of training people to help others on an in-
service basis is one which is wide and heterogeneous. Helpers
are full-time and part-time, paid and voluntary. Employing
organisations are statutory and voluntary. Helpers include
social workers, doctors, counsellors, health visitors and
nurses to name but a few. Different professions and organisations have adopted their own approaches and methodologies.
The trainers themselves often lack any training as trainers.
Their understanding of the educational philosophy, pedagogy
and methodology involved in training is often learned on the
job. Indeed, there is little in the way of published material
about training the trainers; trainers tend to learn through
trial and experience. Yet what has increasingly come to unite
all these varied interests is a move away from didactic,
lecture based educational methods towards a more student
centred approach, utilising the student's own personal experience as a vehicle for learning. The idea of a workshop, a
group of people working together to share experiences and
develop skills neatly encapsulates the pedagogic vehicle which
has come to the fore in recent decades in training people in
helping skills. The prime inspiration for this work has been
the writing of Carl Rogers, the educational correlates of
whose work have been specifically articulated in 'Freedom To
Learn for the 80's' (Rogers 1983).

THE NATURE OF EXPERIENTIAL LEARNING

Experiential learning has been defined elsewhere by one of the
Coping With Crisis Group (Murgatroyd 1982) as having four main
components:-
    1. the learner is aware of the processes which are taking
       place; which are enabling learning to occur,
    2. the learner is involved in a reflective experience
       which enables the person to relate current learning to

past, present and future, even if these time-
relationships are felt rather than thought,
3. personally significant experience and content: what is
being learned and how it is being learned are of
special importance to the person,
4. there is an involvement of the whole self; body,
thoughts, feelings and actions, not just the mind; in
other words the learner as a whole person.

These principles result in the following concrete propositions.
1. Experiential learning is concerned with the experience
of individuals not just with their participation.
Participants are asked to consider and utilise their
own experience as a basis for self understanding and
assessment of their own needs, resources and objectives.
2. The individual participant is regarded as an active
rather than a passive participant in the process of
defining and putting into practice educational agendas
and methodologies.
3. Through this process, power (locus of control) is
shifted away from the teacher in the direction of the
learner. Another way to put this would be to say that
the nature of the teacher-student relationship is
usually asymmetrical; the former has more power than
the latter. In the workshops described in this book,
this asymmetry is reduced. Learners are planning,
carrying out and evaluating their own learning. The
'expert' and the learner engage in a process which is
concerned not with the former transferring facts into
the latter; but rather with facilitating an active
process of learning in the student. It could be described as a move away from a model of education in which
the learner is seen as an empty vessel to be filled
full of facts towards one in which the latter is seen
as a candle to be lit; a potential to be developed.
4. The participant becomes responsible for his or her own
learning. The expert is a resource and a provider of
structure, but learning is seen as taking place when
the learner is trying actively to assimilate external
knowledge into his or her own internal frame of
reference.

We would like to elaborate these points by saying something
about how they are reflected in each of the chapters which
follow. Chapter 2 explores the experience of running workshops
on the subject of coping with stress. The author draws a
distinction between stress perceived as an objective phenomenon
and stress perceived subjectively; that is to say how each
individual comes to identify, understand and experience stress.
While there are many similarities between individuals, each
individual experiences stress in a unique way. The author

3

describes how the focus of the workshop is concerned with
helping individuals to understand, through sharing, what
stress means to each of them as individuals. The structure of
the workshop reflects this emphasis. The basis of the workshop
is established by a series of linked activities through which
individuals are enabled to gain insight first into what it
means to say that stress is experienced, secondly into the
source or origin from which they see this stress as deriving
and thirdly the ways they have of reducing stress. Formal
knowledge is seen as generated by the participants' own work.
Thus, for example, the idea of types of coping strategy derives
from the workshop itself and the efforts of the participants
to understand what stress means to them. The author describes
how more formal academic structure can be arrived at as a
result of using the participants' own experiences and sharing.
In other words, knowledge is constructed through the workshop
rather than being seen as a product presented by an expert to
the unknowing. The experience of the participants is regarded
as an asset through which his or her understanding of both
self and the external world can be increased.

The following chapter is also concerned with stress, in a
specific context, work, but this time with an organisational
rather than an individual focus. It can be described as seeking to promote an understanding of the interactive relationship between experience, reflection and learning. This can be
described diagrammatically as follows:-

Experience ——> Reflection ——> Learning ——> Experience ——>

The workshop can be seen to promote this model of education by
1. structuring the person's reflective experience of stress at
work; 2. providing a model and a language through which experience can be reflected upon and 3. providing an opportunity
for participants to engage in the reflection/learning process
together in a spirit and climate of mutual support. The barriers to experiential learning that arise in this workshop are
of two kinds; 1. those that relate to the personal pain of
learning; 2. those that are about the difficulty of accepting
responsibility for learning about self in front of others. In
order to overcome these problems the workshop design moves
from 'safe' activities to increasingly unsafe ones. Throughout
this process the teacher is seen as needing to exercise monitoring functions so as to maximise learning and minimise undue
distress.

The third workshop account is concerned with training in
basic counselling and communication skills. An important aspect
of this particular workshop is the use of role play, through
which the idea of experiential learning is translated from a
theoretical concept into reality. The author describes how
participants experience at first hand what it feels like to be
involved in a therapeutic encounter. They are also intimately

involved in evaluating the experience. This is concerned not just at the end with looking at what changes the experience of the workshop has brought, but also with encouraging participants to evaluate their own previous experiences of communication or failure to communicate and effectiveness or non-effectiveness in helping relationships. In other words individual self evaluation is an integral aspect of the ongoing process of the workshop. An evaluation at the end is just the final stage of this process. While every workshop account emphasises the need for a clear structure, this one makes the point most explicitly. The objective is to teach specific skills in a defined manner. What is offered to participants can be defined as freedom within structure; self-expression within the limits of clearly signalled structural parameters.

Whereas this account emphasises the area of skills basic to communication and counselling, the following chapter is concerned with the more diffuse concept of helping skills. Moreover, unlike the other chapters, this is concerned with a specific occupational group, Health Visitors. Nevertheless, the principles behind the workshop are similar. The leader describes how she used the workshop as a personal learning project and the chapter illustrates how principles of experiential learning were employed. The approach adopted was again one of freedom within structure, a perspective which was explored with the students at the beginning of the workshop. The issue of the power held respectively by leader and participants receives attention. The author makes it clear that learning is a risky business for all parties concerned. Students were reluctant at times to accept that they were active shapers of their own experiences, as opposed to being the object of influences external to them. The chapter offers a somewhat original conceptual structure of the leader as decision maker and the process of running the workshop as a series of connected decisions. The account of student motivation indicates that it is a multifaceted phenomenon. While students were expected to come to the workshop as part of their Diploma course, the enthusiastic way in which many joined in the activities, indicated an intrinsic motivation to learn more about helping skills as a topic in its own right.

Shooter's chapter on coping with death and bereavement begins with the question, why is a workshop setting necessary? The answer provided is that people seeking help require not words of advice, but an opportunity to express emotional pain. An experiential workshop offers precisely this opportunity. The chapter indicates that for this particular workshop one day has been found to be the optimum length, with a clear break for lunch. This allowed participants to escape temporarily from the group setting if they felt the need for privacy. The day limit avoided the possible threat for participants of things going on forever. This is congruent with the overall aim of providing a good experience of sharing within safe boundaries.

Experiential learning is seen as involving actively challenging people at an emotional level. Without such challenge no change is possible. Given that this is so, it has been important to make clear to potential participants exactly what they might expect from a workshop. The account of the workshop illustrates, like all the chapters in this book, that helpers cannot remain emotionally aloof from the experiences of the event. It follows that there is a need for there to be more than one leader if this is at all possible.

The final workshop account on sexuality emphasises that such workshops are experiential because it is fundamental that what is being learned and assimilated is not information primarily but ways of dealing with problems. Because this cannot effectively be done by didactic teaching, it has to be done through an examination of people's attitudes and perceptions. This is done by looking at early learning experiences of sexuality, becoming immersed in the language of sexuality and sharing of thoughts and ideas with the group about different aspects of sexuality.

The aims of the workshops are seen as being:-
1. to increase the awareness of participant's own sexuality;
2. to increase awareness of others' sexuality, and
3. to be able to discuss sexuality with others.

If one looks at the role of the trainer, it can be seen that this type of workshop involving discussion of a sensitive subject is risky for the trainer, as the group can take the subject where it wishes and this freedom is important for successful workshops. The trainer, therefore, cannot predict what will happen and has to accept or acknowledge the group's feelings.

The chapter exemplifies some of the problems experienced in sexuality workshops. The need to have co-leaders is important because of the defended areas involved in sexuality work. The potential for destructiveness by a leader via a group is certainly present and co-leaders can take the heat out of this, but the relationship and degree of comfort between co-leaders needs to be established prior to the workshop. Confronting resistance within the group is vitally important because this is a mirroring of what participants may be experiencing within their own work situation and if this is not resolved then workshops will not play any useful purpose in these participants' experience. This of course has to be done in a way that enables the leader to keep in contact with the group without lecturing them.

Every chapter helps to establish the practical relevance of experiential learning and the key assumption it makes: that learning about a subject (death, sexuality, stress, communication etc.) cannot be divorced from the process of learning about self. If they are sufficiently open and receptive,

students can learn a great deal about self in areas such as
feelings of learning competence, anxiety about ability to
learn, examination anxiety, or ability to cope with the press-
ures of deadlines for submitting essays. The point is that
learning places the self under the microscope and exposes all
kinds of feelings. Some students may dislike what they see and
deny feelings which emerge by externalising them. They blame
the teacher or the book or the system rather than examine
aspects of self which have emerged. But for the student who is
sufficiently open to look at self, learning offers a big
opportunity for re-evaluation, to put the self into new
relationships with the world.

Our experience is that this process (which is of course a
group as well as an individual experience) is likely to have
major implications not just for the individual but for their
families. So, for example, what participants learn through
studying stress or bereavement or counselling and communication
or sexuality, is taken out of the workshop into a complex
social matrix or network of existing relationships. This may
well produce lasting changes in relationships and lifestyles.
This applies not just to intimate personal relationships, but
also to very traditionally defined professional relationships.
Indeed, our experience has been that participants who have
joined workshops ostensibly stressing their role as emotionally
neutral, white-coated professionals in order to develop skills
or expertise and who explicitly initially disavow any interest
in personal change, find that the experience of participating
in an experiential learning event generates all kinds of feelings of which they had previously been only dimly aware. It is
difficult to ignore such feelings, which by their presence
provoke the subject to looking at themselves. To make this
point allows us to stress that experiential learning is more
than just the physical act of participation. It involves the
whole being of the participant, his or her active intellectual
and emotional participation.

THE ROLE OF THE TRAINER

These four principles have a number of implications for trainers. These are:-
1. Control of the nature and content of learning is shifted away from the trainer towards the student. This
   may involve the tutor in feelings of risk and uncertainty with which he or she may not be familiar;
2. The trainer has to allow students to make mistakes.
   Making mistakes is traditionally perceived as providing
   feedback about the tutor's skills and competence as
   well as about the student's performance. Experiential
   learning, however, is based on the notion that all
   experiences are learning experiences. The tutor,
   therefore, must be clear about who is responsible for

the students' learning and what taking or accepting responsibility means. Some tutors, it can be argued, barely begin to accept any responsibility for the student; certainly not the lecturer who walks in, talks and walks out. The facilitator.does take responsibility in so far as he or she works to develop an awareness of when there is an apparent lack of understanding and, as far as possible, seeks to provide a variety of opportunities for students, if they wish, to remedy their lack of understanding. The tutor assumes that different people have different ways of learning and, therefore, need different types of opportunities. To this extent the tutor can be said to accept responsibility. But in the final resort, responsibility lies with each individual student for the success or otherwise of the learning enterprise in which they are engaged. Unless the tutor is able to accept this fact and to let go, the student is maintained in a position of dependency. This is as unhelpful to the student as the abrogation of all responsibility.

3. Groups need structure, but in experiential learning boundaries have to be negotiated with the participants. These may refer to time, the nature of activities, agenda items or the relationship between tutor and students. Negotiation is not a greatly used skill in more conventional didactic methods, but in experiential learning it becomes crucial.

4. The trainer has to be prepared to become redundant. This may involve learning how to cope with feelings of being unwanted.

5. Sometimes groups coalesce and form an identity through the process of identifying an outsider, against whom they can react. This outsider is frequently the facilitative leader. The trainer has to be able to work through this process and to be sufficiently self aware to acknowledge that the rejection may have more to do with the needs of the group members than with any personal inadequacies in himself or herself.

For all these reasons, running an experiential group involves the leader in taking risks. Instead of being the all-knowing expert, the leader deliberately places himself or herself in a vulnerable position, in a situation where the idea of expert (the knowledgeable parent telling the naive child) is replaced by a process in which the expert becomes facilitator, and to use the language of Transactional Analysis (Berne 1964), Parent is mature enough to become Adult and to help Child become Adult. Integral to this process is that the tutor is involved in it not just as a cerebral component (a disembodied brain) but as a whole person with feelings. Awareness of these feelings is certainly a necessary, even if not a sufficient

condition, for effective workshop functioning. It involves
acknowledgement of areas of self that are potentially frightening and painful such as that one sometimes gets angry or that
one has sexual desires and fantasies or that one sometimes
dislikes people for reasons which are irrational. It's not that
the trainer is expected to be the perfect human being, but that
he or she must have a commitment to understanding himself or
herself. A trainer cannot expect participants to look at themselves in depth unless he or she is prepared to do the same.
Without such a commitment, the tutor will not be able to
disentangle what is happening within a group of people in terms
of differentiating between their needs and his or her needs.
The tutor is, therefore, up-front, aware, exposed, not attempting to defend himself or herself with the structure (shroud) of
expert status.

We referred above to the notion of facilitative leadership
as a necessary but not necessarily sufficient condition of
effective group functioning and it is worthwhile saying a few
more words about this subject at this point. It should be made
quite clear, that facilitation is not a euphemism for anarchy
or for a policy of laissez-faire. The term (often used as
synonymous with the idea of 'enabling') implies a commitment
to a client or student centred form of relationship or to
operating from within the other person's frame of reference.
Yet as most people with experience of leading a workshop group
will testify, this is not the same thing as non-involvement or
non-participating or withdrawing from responsibility for
establishing a structure, framework and boundaries within
which a group of people can work. Indeed, as each chapter in
the book testifies without exception, the workshop in question
is carried out within a clear and well defined structure, the
responsibility for whose establishment, lies with the facilitator as well as the participants. Indeed, that is one of his
or her primary tasks. It is not enough, therefore, just to
describe facilitation as a form of student-centredness without
a prior acknowledgement of the fact that this must take place
within defined limits. This is necessary for the well-being of
both trainer and participants.

What these limits are is a function of how a group of
people came into being, its chosen methods of operation and
ground rules for member interaction, as well as what tasks if
any it has to achieve. In a sense we can describe the answers
to this set of related questions as forming a contract (sometimes explicit, most usually implicit) which group members have
with the group. In the groups described in this book, the goal
or objective or task is usually well formulated: to learn how
to help people to cope with stress, bereavement, sexual problems etc. All group members acknowledge these objectives by the
very act of joining the group. For the facilitator to ignore
these expectations and simply to run the group as say an open
ended encounter group would be to invite disaster and is

certainly not what is meant by facilitation. In practice,
members' expectations represent a critically important dimension in the practice of running any workshop and we would like
to explore this subject further below.

EXPECTATIONS AND CONTRACTS

People are motivated to come to workshops for a variety of
reasons. These include 1. to increase their own knowledge of a
subject area, 2. to hear what experts have to say, 3. to
improve their skills, 4. to be better able to help the people
they work with, 5. to become more self aware, 6. for personal
therapy, 7. to share ideas, 8. to express fears and anxieties,
9. because they feel it will be instrumental in the process of
gaining promotion or a better job, 10. because their line
managers expect them to attend and 11. because they are repre-
senting an organisation. This list is by no means exhaustive,
but it does illustrate the problem faced by the facilitator in
meeting everyone's needs. The person who comes to hear the
expert is likely to have a different set of educational requirements and a different kind of personal commitment to the
workshop from the person who is motivated for example by a
desire to increase self awareness and to promote personal
change.

   Perhaps we can refer to motivation as falling into one of
two categories, either intrinsic or extrinsic. In the case of
the latter, the motivation for attendance can be seen as deriving from outside the individual himself or herself. So for
example, people come to the stress workshop described in this
book because they perceive this as expected from them by their
organisation or because it is seen as a useful pathway towards
promotion or because an intimate friend has insisted on atten-
ance as a basis for the continuation of the friendship. By and
large it can be said that the individual's commitment to the
workshop is likely to be greater the more intrinsic is his or
her motivation. It should of course be appreciated that this
is simply a rough model to help our thinking. In real life,
variables such as motivation are often manifested as a continuum; lots of shades of grey rather than just two discrete
black and white positions. Moreover, motivation (a person's
desire to do something) operates at both a conscious and a
sub-conscious level. So, for example, while at a conscious
level a person may attend a workshop in order to assess how
an organisation can adapt its organisational procedure so as
to better cope with the stress of its members, at a less conscious level that individual may be motivated by a desire to
cope in a more satisfactory way with the stresses of his or
her own life.

   In these ways, therefore, individuals bring to workshops
many different expectations and it is important for the trainer
to assess what these mean in terms of the agenda (programme)

and the methods employed in the workshop. The need to check out expectations cannot be overstressed. If this is not done, the trainer can easily get into what could be described as the 'Chiefs and Indians' syndrome. What happens typically is that the trainer comes to the workshop with a set of expectations derived from prior discussions with those people responsible for organising it, who frequently are themselves not active participants. Participants' needs may be interpreted for example as to run a workshop on counselling skills, or the nature of adult learning or how to cope with stress. However, when one asks the participants themselves what their needs arè, one frequently discovers a considerable divergence between their expressed needs and those needs as articulated by their organisers and managers. This point is made by Hobbs in his chapter in this book. The writer of this chapter had a similar experience of working with community education development workers who were said to need a workshop on adult learning needs and group dynamics. When this was checked out with the participants, what they were really concerned about was the management expectation that the prime criterion of job performance would be the number of groups successfully established. What they wanted, therefore, from the workshop was some understanding of how communities operated, so that they could more accurately assess community needs and thus initiate new groups. Another example concerns a group of teachers concerned with in-service education, whose managers thought they needed a training course in resolution of conflict within groups. However, the workers themselves were more concerned with the lack of definition inherent in their job description and wanted to use the workshop to explore the potential and the limitations inherent in the job.

The expectations which participants bring to a workshop refer not just to their perception of their needs but also to how these needs can be met. We might say that there are expectations about pedagogy or about method as well as about content. This often expresses itself in terms of the participants' desire to be given the 'facts', to be told the 'truth', to see the trainer not as facilitator but as leading expert. What we are talking about here is the reciprocal of what we referred to above as the risks inherent for trainers in adopting a facilitative role. Just as there is a risk for trainers, so there is a corresponding risk for participants. This is that they will not be able to remain hidden in a passive fashion but will actively be called upon to reveal aspects of self experience about which they may feel vulnerable or defensive. This may not operate at a conscious level. We have dozens of examples of workshops where participants have been told beforehand, often in written form, that they will be expected to accept responsibility for their own learning, yet where participants have found this hard to come to terms with in practice. In such situations, participants find the idea of an active form

of participation, in which they are expected to explore the
interface between ideas presented and their own experience, too
threatening to contemplate. The result is often resistance,
directed usually initially at the trainer for not taking on the
role of expert. Such experiences indicate that the idea of
'accepting responsiblity for one's own learning' often means
little to many participants at an emotional level. While it
may sound all right intellectually, the first attempts to
invoke the philosophy, to translate an idea into operational
practice may provoke strong defensive reactions. The author
recently worked with a local authority group of eighteen managers, selected according to their potential for promotion to
the most senior positions. The day workshop on coping with stress
came some nine months through a one year course. At the workshop it soon became clear that there was major resistance
within the group to the idea of an experiential workshop, what
they wanted was skills. They were not prepared, as a group, to
consider the appropriateness of their request to the subject
areas in question. What was clear to the trainer (the author)
was that this resistance had developed over the nine month
period and during many meetings, yet the group and the organiser still persisted in the rhetoric that they were involved
in experiential learning and accepting responsibility for their
own learning. No attempt had been made to confront this fantasy.

COPING WITH DIFFICULTIES

This example raises the question of what the facilitator might
do when conflict of expectations of this nature is experienced.
While there are no simple answers to this question and each
situation must be assessed on its own merits, there are a
number of guidelines which can be offered.
1.  It is absolutely crucial to have a clear answer to the
    question of is it something about me (the facilitator)
    or is it something about this group that is causing
    the blockage? No matter how extensive our skills and
    experience, we all as facilitators have our own defend-
    ed areas and sometimes, perhaps quite unexpectedly a
    group of people can activate these defences. In such
    situations we may have to face up to the possibility
    that the problem lies with the facilitator rather than
    with the participants and that progress is dependent
    upon him or her acknowledging and responding actively
    to these defences. This is just one reason, though a
    critical one, why every workshop should preferably have
    co-leaders if at all possible. Between them two people
    can check out their perceptions of what is happening
    against each other.
2.  Sometimes, however, it becomes clear, as in the example
    above, that the problem lies with the group participants
    not with the trainer. In this case, a number of options

are available. The first is to confront the group with
its resistance. This is likely to involve the trainer
becoming the recipient of angry feelings, as the calm
and equilibrium that the group has established in order
to defend itself from self examination is disturbed.
In the example above this anger continued for the whole
day and imposed considerable stress upon the trainer.
The fact that he did not have a co-leader (for economic
reasons) contributed to his discomfort and made his
task that much more difficult. It could of course be
argued that the trainer was unwise to have taken on the
leadership of this workshop if it were not possible to
pay for a co-leader to work with him. The notion of
confronting the blocked situation is akin to the sense
in which in individual counselling, the counsellor will
find it necessary to raise the subject of the relationship between client and counsellor, if the client
appears to have a negative perception of the counsellor.
In this way, the blocked situation with its stuck feelings is described as being confronted. Clearly it does
not mean banging the arms of one's chair or acting in
an aggressive, frightening or threatening fashion.

3. It is often, however, difficult to confront the group
in the manner outlined above. In the case of the example already quoted, this was a difficult option to take
because of the expectations of the organisers who were
employing the trainer for the day. Their expectation
was for a smooth running event in which motivation was
seen to be high and in which clear evidence of learning
would take place and its implications for the organisation acknowledged. In the event it became clear to the
trainer that the contract he had with the organisers
was an unfair one in the sense that important details
about the history of the group had not been revealed to
him (though perhaps the organisers were not even aware
of them) before he had agreed to undertake the task in
hand. In this kind of situation, one may sometimes
simply need to accept the reality of the situation as
seen by participants and to don the mantle of expert.
Whatever the decision one takes, the example illustrates that expectations and contracts do exist in the
minds of organisers, participants and trainers. If
there are any differences between the three sets of
expectations, these will inevitably express themselves
in the workshop. The moral is that the task of running
a workshop begins long before the participants ever
get together and involves the trainer in agreeing a
contract which will ensure that he or she understands
and is able to meet the expectations imposed on him or
her. This sometimes means that the trainer must be
quite explicit about what he or she expects from

participants in order to clarify expectations to them.

While we have talked above about how to handle conflict in
workshops, it is necessary to be clear that conflict provides
a vehicle for learning and is not necessarily bad or destructive. Indeed, sometimes workshops may even involve the active
creation of conflictual situations (as in a role playing sim-
ulation about decision making) so that participants can explore
what conflict feels like in a structured, controlled context.

## CONCLUDING COMMENTS

Experiential learning is not likely to be an easy option,
either for the learner or for the trainer. Even in the act of
engaging group members in what are often euphemistically called
'ice-breakers' or 'warming-up' exercises, sensitive personal
areas are likely to be confronted. Just being asked to think
about our first name by itself often provokes strong feelings
about self image and relationships with parents. But paradoxically the fact that experiential workshops are concerned with
feelings provides the energy and the potential through which
learning is facilitated. The experiential workshop assumes that
people feel as well as think and their concern with the whole
person is their primary characteristic. This above all else is
what identifies every workshop described in this book.

Yet as we have seen, the enterprise involves risk both for
the participants and the trainers. The latter can no longer
rely on handing down tablets of stone. Indeed, he or she must
find methods of sticking with the needs of participants as they
are exposed to the awful uncertainty that there may be no tablets of stone, or absolute truths and, therefore, no experts.
The trainer must, therefore, be prepared to work with the
dynamics of a group as it comes to terms with the full implications of this fact; as it begins to experience the implications of accepting responsibility for its own learning.

When these risks are practised in the context of the
settings described in this book, they can be seen to be both
significant and real. No trainer or participant can be expected to engage in a workshop on stress, death or sexuality without being prepared to explore these areas in the context of
his or her life. The results may be painful or creative of
anxiety and uncertainty as old defences are exposed. It is
hardly surprising, therefore, that each author, without exception emphasises the need to tread cautiously, to be sensitive
to what is happening to self and others, to display the quality
of immediacy (stay in the here and now), and to work whenever
possible with a co-leader (or leaders). In short an experiential workshop can be represented as a process in which people
come together to learn not just about subject content but about
self. Each workshop described in the book can be represented
as an attempt to facilitate this process of self development.

Experiential Learning in Workshops

REFERENCES

Berne, E. (1964) Games People Play, Penguin, Harmondsworth
Murgatroyd, S.J. (1982) 'Experiential Learning and the Person
    in Pursuit of Psychology', Education Section Review
    (British Psychological Society), 6,2, pp. 112-117
Rogers, C.R. (1983) Freedom To Learn for the '80's,
    Charles E. Merrill, Columbus, Ohio

Chapter Two

COPING WITH STRESS : A FRAMEWORK FOR A WORKSHOP[1,2]

RAY WOOLFE

## MODELS OF STRESS AND COPING

Traditionally, stress has been perceived as a force or forces
which exist(s) externally to the individual, somewhere out in
the world and which exerts pressure upon the individual. The
model is analogous to that used by engineers to describe a
situation in which a force acts upon a physical object and
generates a strain in that object. Stress is thus essentially
seen as an input measure of an event external to the individual.
One result of this approach has been the generation of a number
of scales designed to measure the stress potential of particular events, of which the best known is that of Holmes and
Rahe (1967). In this particular scale, to give but a few examples, the Death of a Spouse is given a stress value of 100
points, Divorce 73, Marriage 50, Retirement 45, down to Change
in Residence 20, Christmas 12 and Minor Violations of the Law
11. While this approach clearly has some value, without any
doubt death or divorce or house moving clearly have the potential to be stress producing events, it is also equally clear
that no two individuals react in exactly the same way to any
given event. Some people seem to thrive generally in potentially stressful situations, while others appear to have less
ability to adapt and to cope.

Other writers, therefore, have focused upon output as well
as input in asking how an individual responds or adapts to an
outside stressor (a stimulus-response model). An important
worker in this tradition is Caplan (1964 and 1968) who emphasises the individuals' desire to maintain balance in their
lives (he calls it 'homeostasis'). Stress arises when the
individual is unable to cope with a situation which generates
arousal with the result that levels of arousal continue to
grow. This produces anxiety or stress. More accurately, as the
discrepancy between desired arousal and felt arousal increases,
the feeling of tension the individual experiences also
increases.

More recent work emphasises the importance of examining

16

the interaction between environmental stimulus (stressor) and
the reacting individual. In fact the notion of a stimulus or
stressor must be seen as part of a reactive or more accurately
an interactive situation. This model is essentially the one we
follow in this chapter in which the emphasis is on stress and
coping as a subjective rather than objective phenomenon. While
we do not deny that some people may be more prone to experience
stress than others either because of personality type or because of the environmental context in which they live, our concern is phenomenological: with how people come to understand,
experience and cope with stress. The model is associated with
Lazarus (Lazarus and Launier, 1981) and perceives the individual in a transactional relationship with the environment; a
person-enviroment relationship in an adaptational encounter
(Lazarus 1978). Stress occurs when there is a misfit between
the characteristics of the person and the environment. Coping
is the process of working towards a state of fit between the
two. The model can be described as cognitive as well as phenomenological. By this, we mean that emotions (and stress) are
seen as products of cognitions, through the way in which individuals appraise the situation in which they find themselves.
Appraisal in fact is a key concept. The individual works
through a process of appraisal, by means of a 'how am I doing'
set of questions and thereby makes decisions about the adequacy
of coping mechanisms employed. Coping is, therefore, seen not
as a fixed structural property of the person but as a transaction which itself transforms that environment. Put simply,
therefore, we are suggesting that stress resides neither in
the environment nor in the person, but in the interaction between the two. This view has the important consequence of inves-
ting emphasis upon the individual as an active factor in both
creating and coping with his or her experiences.

   This model has a number of consequences for workshop practice. In particular, it informs the need to facilitate a situation in which each individual can be allowed to make a self
appraisal of his or her own techniques for understanding and
coping with stress. Pedagogically this sets clear limits on
the use of didactic methods of teaching and emphasises the
process of student centred learning. In terms of content it
directs us towards examining the relationship between thinking
and feeling as a central feature of the workshop. While
Lazarus' model perceives emotions as a product of cognitions,
it recognises that the relationship between the two is strongly
interactive. Whatever the source of emotions, once experienced
they clearly influence thinking and behaviour. Anxiety for
example is consistently reported by participants as affecting
thinking processes, often in the area of creating states of
cognition confusion. This creates further anxiety and so the
interactive cycle continues. For this reason the structure of
the workshop is strongly influenced by the concepts of thinking
and feeling and their outcomes in terms of behaviour and body

(physical states). This can be represented diagrammatically as shown in figure 1.

Figure 1: The relationship between thinking, feeling, behaviour and body

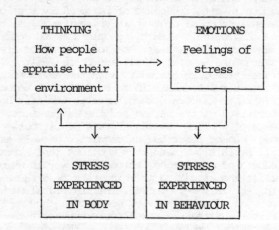

WORKSHOP STRUCTURE

The remainder of this chapter outlines the experience of the Open University's Coping With Crisis Research and Training Group in running workshops during the past five years on the theme of coping with stress. The framework described represents the distilled result of some three dozen workshops ranging in length from an afternoon (one session) to a whole weekend (four sessions). In other words the model which we now follow has evolved and developed as the direct result of experience gained. This chapter presents the contents of a full two day workshop (comprising four three-hour sessions) but in essence the shorter workshops follow a similar pattern. While the amount of work covered may be less, the philosophy and the objectives remain largely the same.

These can be described as fourfold:
1. to increase the awareness of participants of what experiencing stress means to them, using the thinking, feeling, behaviour and body dimensions,
2. to encourage them to explore the conditions under which they experience stress,
3. to help participants to focus upon their existing coping mechanisms for dealing with stress,
4. to present to participants, through the experience of group membership, a range of coping mechanisms which

offers them an opportunity to increase their repertoire
of coping skills.

The philosophy underlying these objectives is that there is a
need to attempt to reconcile two potentially conflicting
approaches to dealing with coping with stress. On the one hand,
it is possible to approach the subject in the primarily humanistic terms of increasing self awareness without too much concern about specific coping skills. On the other hand, it is
possible to approach it as located in a set of specific coping
skills, without too much concern about the level of self
awareness embedded in the practice of these skills. The more
experience we have gained in the workshops, the more we have
found it necessary to adopt an eclectic approach. Partly this
reflects the fact that participants come to the workshop with
different needs and partly it reflects a degree of pragmatism
which suggests that the two approaches are more easily separated in theory than in practice. It also, however, reflects
our own personal philosophy that the presentation of skills
without awareness is de-humanising, while a focus upon awareness without attention to skills overlooks the latter's value
as a practical helping mechanism. We have articulated this
philosophy in Murgatroyd and Woolfe (1982) as a 'commitment to
both eclectic helping interventions within the community and
with individuals and to our search for simple models of crisis,
change and transition which help in the understanding of the
pain of personal crisis'.

More specifically we would describe our approach as
encompassed within what Dryden (1984) refers to as 'technical
eclecticism', as being more concerned with practical rather
than theoretical issues, and as expressing our concern with
the question 'what technique works for whom, and under which
particular conditions'. Dryden suggests that perhaps the best
example of technical eclecticism is Lazarus's 'Multi Modal
Therapy', which systematically covers seven basic modalities
of human functioning and dysfuntioning in therapy: behaviour,
affect, sensation, imagery, cognition, interpersonal relationships and drug-taking/physiological - hence the acronym BASIC
ID. While we have not so far followed these modalities in the
methodical fashion outlined by Lazarus (Lazarus 1981), our
work has been informed by this approach and is likely to develop further in this direction.

The Participants
Participants have come from a wide variety of professional
backgrounds. Our experience has been that social workers,
nurses (particularly health visitors), teachers, psychologists
have been forthcoming in large numbers while other groups such
as doctors (particularly G.P.s) and clergy have proved more
difficult to attract. Many of the workshops have been mixed,
but some have been provided at the request of particular

organisations and occupational groups and, therefore, have been more homogeneous in composition. Our practice suggests that a dozen is an optimum number although we have operated with less and with more (if sufficient leadership resources existed). For the open workshops, participants have by and large been self-selected as a result of local advertisement, more or less on a first come first served category. We normally ask people to make a financial contribution of say £12 for a whole weekend; correspondingly less for the unwaged. It has not been our practice to send any preparatory material to prospective participants, other than the information provided on the application form. This draws attention to the four objectives previously outlined and indicates the participative, experiential basis of the workshop. In the case of the single occupation groups (block bookings) the leaders have some ideas of what needs participants bring to and their expectations of the workshop. However, even here caution is desirable. Experience suggests that what the 'Indians' expect or want is often substantially different from what the 'Chiefs' suggest they need or want. So the first part of every workshop is always centrally concerned with gleaning information about what participants themselves expect and desire from it.

Of course the more heterogeneous a group is, the more difficult this task becomes and the more complex it is to balance what may well be conflicting needs. For example, many of the people who have attended the workshops have themselves been experiencing considerable stress and even crisis at the time and have seen the workshops as an opportunity to work at resolving their immediate problems. For others, their primary motivation has been to discover techniques which they can use in helping their own clients. Our approach to such potential conflict has been as follows. At the outset of each workshop, we have made clear to participants that all therapeutic training begins with the exploration of the 'self' of the therapist, but that this poses a potential problem for the group. This concerns the extent to which the use of the group by any individual for the purpose of catharsis is likely to lead to the group as a whole being helped or hindered in the primary task for which members have contracted. We ask the group members to be sensitive to this 'problem' and to take some responsibility for determining the direction taken by the group. In practice, the leaders (of whom there have almost always been at least two) have, as one of their main tasks, a need to develop a careful understanding of both the expectations and contracts that exist within the group. For this reason the leaders have to be consistently concerned with simple questions of group dynamics like who is in this group now; what brought them here; what expectations do they have; what are the dynamics of the group; who is strong and who is in need of support? The extent of their on going concern with these and related questions will be a function of the leaders'

familiarity with the group and the group's familiarity with
each other. Throughout the remainder of the chapter, the need
for the leaders to remain cognizant of group dynamics will be
treated implicitly rather than explicitly. However, this in no
way should be taken as underestimating the importance of what
is happening in the group. Over the years we have found that
our experience of encounter groups has provided a useful source
of activities in helping groups to warm up, reduce controls,
increase interaction, express trust and openness, experience
a sense of fun and enjoyment, and generally work together
harmoniously. Details of such activities can be found in two
classical books on encounter groups by Rogers (1969) and in
Schutz (1967).

Group leaders have all been members of the Coping With
Crisis Research and Training Group and have come from a range
of occupations (university lecturing, counselling psychology,
clinical psychology, social work, psychiatry and sociology).
However, they have all had a common commitment to the type of
eclecticism outlined above which emphasises the importance of
the question, what works for whom and in what conditions and
acknowledging individual needs while working in a group setting.
Workshops have been planned collectively and evaluated in the
same way, thus ensuring an ongoing process of assessment, sup-
ervision and development.

Session 1
After an initial period of warming up and getting to know each
other, the first of the four sessions (lasting until the end
of the morning of the first day) has focused around three
consecutive but linked activities concerned to develop awareness about three related issues:-
1.  What do we understand or mean when we say that we are
    experiencing stress? For each individual, the question
    posed is 'how do you experience stress?'
2.  From where does this stress emanate? The emphasis here
    is on the source of the triggers which cause stress
    for the individual.
3.  What strategies are available for coping with stress?

We have sometimes found it useful or even necessary to remind
participants, before getting into these activities, that the
contract we have with them is not to provide a tutorial-like
input. Rather we have indicated that the experiences of those
present are real for them and a rich source of sharing and
interacting with others. Moreover, this is a workshop in which
discovery and the processes of discovery are themselves tools
for coping.

In the first activity, participants are asked to complete
the grid in figure 2 as a small group activity. The overall
group is broken down into sub-groups of three or four. People
are encouraged to work with persons they do not know as well

as those they do, and to change groups and work with different
people as the workshop progresses. The task of the group in
this activity is not to agree on a consensus list, but to
ensure that the range of experiences which count as 'stress'
for the participants are fully expressed. To this end, the
grid is drawn up on a large sheet of paper and entries noted
down in what appears to be the most relevant cell. The technique of brainstorming is encouraged; that is to say participants are encouraged to get down anything which comes into their
heads before it is censored or filtered. Each group has its own
chart, so that at the end of the activity, a number of charts
are available for comparison. There is no group leader. Each
person is provided with their own felt pen. If a group leader
emerges then that itself is a topic for discussion.

Figure 2: The experience of stress in different states

|  | FEELING | THINKING | BEHAVIOUR | BODY |
|---|---|---|---|---|
| MILD STRESS |  |  |  |  |
| STRONG STRESS |  |  |  |  |

During the process of chart completion, the activity usually
raises questions about mild and strong stress as a continuum
rather than as a dichotomy. It also raises questions about the
links between cognitive, affective and physical states. Participants note that a pain in the shoulder is often linked to a
lack of concentration or feeling of anxiety or inability to
act purposefully. We have found it useful, after the grids
have been completed, to place them side by side on a wall and
to hold a plenary discussion about the findings. The discussion
can focus around such issues as what are the most common
indicators of stress and what are its most common effects? The
mild/strong distinction offers the opportunity to make the
point that at low levels, stress may well be a positive raiser
of adrenalin, a 'turn-on' or a motivator. Coping may thus be
related to the individual's ability not to reduce stress to a
zero level, but to maintain it at a low level of arousal.

It should also be noted that each individual has his or
her own threshold of desired arousal. The idea of reversal
theory is useful in this context and if appropriate can be
drawn to the attention of the participants. Within reversal
theory, individuals are seen to have two preferred states for
variables such as arousal, serious-mindedness and impulsiveness.

These two states have been labelled telic and paratelic. In the former state the individual sees himself or herself as highly serious minded, goal directed and seeking to avoid excessive arousal. In the latter state the individual sees himself or herself as seeking arousal because it's pleasurable. People reverse between these two states. The implication for our understanding of stress is that the relationship between arousal and anxiety may not be, as it has traditionally been supposed, linear. Murgatroyd (1981) offers a 'bi-variate' model indicating that high levels of arousal may provoke anxiety if an individual is in a telic state, but may be regarded as both exciting and pleasurable if that individual is in the paratelic state. To spell it out, therefore, one can say that in the telic state, relaxation is pleasant (low arousal) and anxiety is unpleasant (high arousal). Conversely, in the paratelic state, boredom is unpleasant (low arousal) and excitement is pleasant (high arousal). If we follow through this argument into work on stress reduction, logic would suggest that any individual in a paratelic state would for instance find relaxation therapy actually increasing rather than reducing his or her stress level. Similarly the telic individual may well find that attempts to get him or her to have fun actually increases levels of stress. Coping with stress, therefore, is not simply a matter of arousal reduction and this point would seem to have relevance in thinking about how anxious individuals are eased into this session. The value of reversal theory is that it helps to guide counsellors and therapists in their selection of diverse therapeutic techniques. Dryden (1984 op cit.) has described the approach adopted by reversal theory as 'structural eclecticism' and it is described fully by Murgatroyd and Apter (1984).

So far as the content of the boxes in figure 2 is concerned, participants find that while they may each experience stress in a unique fashion, there are many areas of overlap with the experience of others. Moreover they find it therapeutic to talk about what may be a painful subject in a trusting and accepting environment. For our part, we have ceased to be surprised by the variety of material generated. Below we have provided just a few examples of the responses offered.

| | |
|---|---|
| Thinking:- | Mental blocks; taking the easy option; diversification; day-dreaming; not being able to switch-off; inability to think straight; confusion; inhibiting creativity; rigidity; inability to understand new ideas. |
| Feeling:- | Depressed; frustrated; short-tempered; irritable; inadequate; angry; withdrawn; anxious; apathetic; humourless; disillusioned. |
| Behaviour:- | Clock watching; withdrawal from company; violence; inflexibility; attention seeking; malingering; shouting and yelling; alcoholic |

excess; indecisive; wanting to talk;
confrontation; smoking; exercise; more sex;
less sex; insomnia.

Body:- Tired; headaches; need to urinate/defecate;
shaking; palpitation; muscular aches; spasms;
skin rashes; twitching.

This is just a small random sample of what people admit to and
it is worthy of note that when we have asked groups of teachers
to note down the characteristics of troublesome or 'maladjust-
ed' pupils, their list bears remarkable similarities to the
characteristics which our participants claim to experience
when under stress. It includes such features as shouting at
others, aggressive behaviour, withdrawn behaviour, lack of
social skills, inability to concentrate and so on.

More and more the feeling/thinking/behaviour/body distinction has come to form both the central theoretical and
practical framework of the workshop. In the early days we had
concentrated upon a self-help/working with others distinction
as a basis for developing the workshop, but gradually this has
been replaced by the differentiation noted above. By the end
of this activity, we assume that participants have an understanding of the idea that stress is a subjective phenomenon;
it is how each individual experiences it, that determines what
stress means to that individual. Given that this is so, participants can be asked to focus on the next activity, which is
concerned with where this stress emanates from. Or to put it
another way, what are the sources of the triggers which cause
stress for the individual? Once again, participants are asked
to fill in a pre-prepared chart in their small groups. This
asks them to note down each source of stress and to locate it
in others, the environment or self. The chart (adapted from
Bond and Kilty 1982) is shown in figure 3.

Figure 3: Stress and its sources

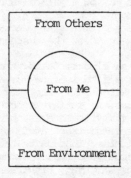

As before, individuals are encouraged to brainstorm. The aim

is not to negotiate with others, but to log all possible
sources of stress for each individual. The more that participants get involved in this activity the more they find that the
diagram becomes characterised by arrows and direction markers.
These reflect the fact that the boundaries are highly artificial. So, for example, participants regularly report smoking
and fouling of pavements by dogs as sources of stress; the
former is usually located in 'others' and the latter in 'the
environment'. However, some reflection reveals that, once the
problem is owned, it can also be located in the 'me' box. While
I may blame smokers or dog owners for causing me stress, the
problem lies ultimately in my perception of smoke or fouled
pavements, perhaps as potential carriers of disease and illness.

Once the problem is accepted as 'mine', it is possible to
do something about it; sometimes involving changing 'my' perceptions and sometimes trying to change the social context.
There is rarely any shortage of material for the 'self' box.
Many participants recognise that it is their own desire to be
loved, or for recognition by bosses or peers, or to experience
excitement, or to satisfy unrealistic self expectations etc.
that causes them stress. Many of these inner needs derive from
messages learned and internalised in childhood and carried over
into adult life. The more that participants recognise the
source of their need for love, approval, esteem etc. the more
they have something tangible on which to work in order to
reduce the stress they are experiencing in the present. A
small sample of the material which emerges is reproduced below:

| From Me:- | Desire for control; desire to be loved/wanted; strong achievement motivation; need for reassurance; high personal standards; personal insecurity; inability to express feelings. |
| From Others:- | Relatives or friends or workmates making unrealistic demands; people being rude; aggressive; unkind; unpleasant; dominating; rejecting. |
| From Environment:- | Dogs; cats; smoking; travelling on trains; planes; buses; cars; politics; the threat of nuclear war; vandalism and delinquency; unemployment; news-papers; the Church. |

An interesting exercise is to encourage the development of
links across the three categories. It illustrates how frequently stress is caused by the individual's unwillingness or inability to own or internalise a particular type of experience or
environment context. The activity provides an opportunity to
address questions such as what are the most dominant sources of
stress? Many participants have found it therapeutic to compare

notes about work as a stressor. One point which has emerged again and again is that the role in which professionals see themselves as cast, the white-coated, emotionally neutral person distanced from clients, which is supposed to shield them from emotional involvement, is one which paradoxically causes them enormous stress. Because they are supposed not to become involved in the client's problems, they report repression of feelings like pain, guilt and anxiety in their dealings with ill health, illness, accident, relationship difficulties and bereavement. The workshops have provided countless opportunities for professionals to acknowledge that helping other people is itself a stressful experience. Many who have come to workshops to find out how to help others to reduce stress find that an understanding of their own stress is a primary prerequisite.

The third and last of the three linked activities for the morning session of day one allows participants to move forward positively from considering the experience of stress to the experience of coping. Once again a chart is provided on which participants denote coping strategies. While originally we provided a chart divided into Adaptive and Maladaptive Strategies, we have gradually preferred to offer groups a blank piece of paper simply entitled 'Coping Strategies'. This allows them to elicit for themselves the fact that alcohol or sexual activity or shouting or exercise or creative activity or a thousand other ways of coping with stress are adaptive or maladaptive, depending on the extent to which each individual employs them and the effect they have on that individual's self image and relationships. Against each strategy, individuals may be encouraged to note first whether they have any skills in the area which they might wish to share with other participants and secondly whether they have an interest in learning more about a particular strategy or approach.

The list of strategies is absolutely enormous. It includes such items as the following:-

Strategies for Coping:- Shouting; swearing; hard work; physical effort; sport; sex (more or less); violence; getting away; alcohol; absenteeism; daydreaming; withdrawal from social life; complaining; knitting; talking; sharing; eating; head banging; not eating; smoking; arguing; gardening.

At this point, lunch is taken. Our policy has always been to encourage people to bring provisions which can be eaten on a sharing basis. At the very least, we hope that participants will eat in rather than go out. Group leaders have always taken part in this process with the other group members. At the same time, because we rely on flexibility, particularly in the

remaining three sessions, we think it is valuable for the
leader (or leaders) to find a certain amount of time on their
own in which they can reflect on the previous session, assess
progress, relax and unwind, and clarify the possibilities and
the shape which the next sessions might take.

## Session 2

When we began the workshop, we played the remaining three sessions very much by ear and this is still the case. We attempt to
take account of our resources as well as the resources available in individual participants and the interests expressed,
and generally to be sensitive to the needs of the group and of
individuals within it. Already by this point of the workshop,
particular individuals have frequently expressed a wish to
explore further some aspect of their life, past or present and
we attempt to structure the workshop so that space can be
found to meet these expressed needs. Beyond this, we have a
wide range of techniques at our disposal which we believe are
useful in coping with stress. These include relaxation training, assertiveness, cognitive re-structuring, co-counselling,
guided fantasy, gestalt and meditation. In the early days, we
delved somewhat haphazardly into these techniques, using them
rather as a pot-pourri. We believe it is true to say that
increasingly our use of these techniques has become more
precise, integrated, lucid and relevant to the subject of
stress. What we have now, therefore, is less of a pot-pourri
and more of a logically coherent approach to looking at stress,
using a variety of techniques, employing participants' own
skills and taking account of their expressed needs.

To begin the afternoon we regularly employ a high energy
children's game known as 'Mixed Veg' or 'Railway Stations'.
Each person takes the name of a vegetable (or railway station).
In a circle, seats are provided for all but one participant (a
volunteer) who stands in the middle. This person calls out the
names of two or more vegetables (or stations). These persons
have to change seats without allowing the person in the middle
to grab a seat. The essence of the game is speed. The person
in the middle is allowed to call out 'Mixed Veg' ('all change')
in which case everyone has to change seats. The game is remarkable in raising the energy level, which is usually fairly low
after lunch, so that participants feel more willing to work.
It is a particularly relevant activity in a number of ways.
First, it demonstrates in action one way of coping with stress,
namely physical activity. Secondly, because it changes the
atmosphere of the group, it demonstrates the link between physical and emotional states. Thirdly, it demonstrates the value
of play in changing psychological states.

At this point, we ask participants to sit down and we
begin to integrate the morning's activity with what is to come.
If appropriate, we point to the paradigm of coping strategies
suggested by Pearlin and Schooler (1978) which we find useful

as an aid to our thinking. They begin by drawing a distinction between tactics and strategy. A strategy is the scheme a person adopts in order to cope with some specific stressful event, whilst a tactic is the person's way of implementing this scheme. Pearlin and Schooler suggest that there are essentially three strategies for coping. These are 1. strategies aimed at preventing situations developing as crisis or stress - an 'anticipatory' strategy, 2. strategies aimed at creating a buffer between the person and the stressful environment, so as to prevent the full effects of the stress being experienced - a 'buffer' strategy, 3. the strategy of coping with a stressful event by learning to manage the feelings and thoughts experienced - a 'crisis-management' strategy.

Anticipatory coping is used by a great many people, for example, psychoprophylaxis (psychological preparation for the prevention of pain) is taught to pregnant mothers in order to ease pain during childbirth. Another example refers to a couple attempting to cope with a relationship problem by negotiating about it. Anticipatory coping sounds ideal, but in practice is difficult to implement for a number of reasons. First, it requires the accurate identification of the potential source of stress. This is not always easy. For example, in marriage it is often difficult to find the specific feature which is creating stress. Secondly, even if a source is identified, individuals sometimes lack the skills to transform it. Thirdly, even if identified and transformed, resultant change may well generate problems elsewhere. For example, working harder to overcome problems at work may create stress in one's private life. Fourthly, some situations such as living with illness or handicap may simply not lend themselves to such forms of coping. Many methods for coping with stress focus upon teaching anticipatory coping. These include relaxation therapy and meditation, assertiveness training and transactional analysis. Reference should also be made to anticipatory grief work in anticipation of death, which doesn't lessen the pain of death, but does decrease the chances of the resulting process of coping, getting stuck and going wrong.

The buffer strategy aims to inhibit the effects of the stressful situation even though the situation itself has developed and does exist. In other words, what is involved here is the reinterpretation of an event so that its effects are perceived as innocuous rather than harmful. Perhaps the most common example is denial that a problem exists. For example, a marital problem is pushed under the carpet with the rationalisation that it doesn't really matter. Denial should not be interpreted in a totally negative light. For example, it may be valuable in the short run in preventing an individual being overwhelmed by a crisis (see Murgatroyd and Woolfe 1982). Another example of buffering is repression or selective perception. For example, the pain of death of a loved one is reduced by perceiving it as involving the end of the sick person's suffering. A third buffer strategy involves reaction-formation, that is doing the opposite of what is thought or felt, but doing it unconsciously. This results in,for example,a sexually repressed person coping with 'dangerous' sexual feelings by actively campaigning against pornography, prostitution etc. For example, a short term response to unemployment may be to reflect about the freedom one now has relative to ex-colleagues still in work. While the buffer strategy may be valuable in the short run, its use of defence mechanisms in the cause of selective perception, denial and repression of painful thoughts and feelings may generate problems in the longer term. Cognitive restructuring of irrational thoughts may be seen as an example of this type of strategy in action.

The crisis-management strategy is concerned with easing the discomfort caused by stress. Such a strategy makes use of any tactic that seems likely to reduce the level of tension. Thus relaxation therapy may be practised for this purpose as well as to futher anticipatory coping, thus illustrating the point that the activity itself represents the tactic, but that it is the use to which it is put which represents the strategy.

This theoretical framework offers participants a conceptual scheme whereby they can attempt to locate the various strategies discussed in the previous session as well as the techniques developed in the workshop. However, the primary conceptual scheme around which we continue to work is the feeling/thinking/behaviour/body distinction. We have found that the links across the four areas are clear and apparent and that the relationship between thinking and feeling is a crucial one for the person. Over the years there has been a long running debate within psychology and psychiatry about the relationship between cognition and affect in both normal and pathological states. Increasingly it is recognised that in both conditions the sequence is one of perception-cognition-emotion, though we ourselves prefer the notion of circularity. Beck (1971) points out that the difference between normal and pathological lies in the way the pathological state is characterised by internal processes which distort the stimulus situation. While the humanistic tradition has tended to downgrade the role of cognition and upgrade the importance of the affect, we believe that there are good reasons for starting with the role of cognition in stress creation and reduction. This belief is rooted not just in the present state of our knowledge but also in the fact that in our society, the use of thinking as a primary tool through which to reflect upon our own actions is a dominating one. In this chapter we have offered an account of the theory which underpins our actions although in the actual workshop the discussions of theory are much less explicit. The emphasis is upon the participants themselves making the links. If theory helps then it is relevant and vice versa.

We move on, therefore, into the area of cognition and the idea of Cognitive Restructuring. If we can change the ways we think about things that cause us stress, they become less stressful. Our aim is not to demonstrate rational or rational-emotive therapy or even to suggest that we approve of its theory or methodology, but rather to draw from it some aspect which will enable participants to think about stress. We have found the 'ABCDE' approach useful, where A stands for activating event; B for beliefs about this event (rational and irrational); C for the consequences of holding these beliefs; D for disputing and challenging the irrational idea; and E for alternative thoughts. How we tackle the activity varies from workshop to workshop, but typically we ask individuals to write down on a piece of paper the details of a situation which causes them stress. We ask them to describe the situation in as much detail as possible including their beliefs about the event and the consequences of holding such beliefs. Basically this is the ABC stages of the sequence. Below is an example, adapted from Davis, Eshelman and McKay (1980).

A. <u>Activating Event</u> - A friend cancelled a date with me.
B. <u>Beliefs</u> - 1. Rational - She's under a lot of pressure at work right now. She hasn't much free time.
        2. Irrational - I'm worthless. Nobody wants to be with me. I'll be lonely tonight.
C. <u>Consequences</u> - I was depressed...., was moderately anxious.
D. <u>Disputing and Challenging the Irrational Ideas</u>
        1. Select the irrational idea. I'm worthless. Nobody wants to be with me. I'll be lonely.
        2. Is there any rational support for the idea? No!
        3. What evidence exists for the falseness of the idea? I have lots of friends of both sexes.
        4. Does any evidence exist for the truth of the idea? No! I've talked myself into feeling depressed.
        5. What is the worst thing that could happen to me? I'll spend one lonely night.
        6. What good things might occur? I could feel more self-reliant and realise that I do have inner resources.
E. <u>Alternative Thoughts</u> - I'm O.K. I'll make myself a nice meal - read and have a warm bath. I'm good at being alone.
  <u>Alternative Emotions</u> - O.K. I feel a little disappointed, but it's not the end of the world and I can have quite a nice quiet, restful evening by myself.

After each person has listed his or her A to C responses on a

piece of paper, participants work in pairs to discuss each
other's case with an emphasis on D and E. The objective is on
the listener 1. identifying the demands made by the speaker on
themselves and others - expressed in 'ought', 'should', 'must'
statements and 2. encouraging the speaker to dispute and cont-
radict these and other irrational beliefs. Elements of co-
counselling practice can be identified here. For example, the
process of talking about the thoughts, feelings and actions of
situations where stress is experienced is the 'literal descriptions' phase, while the role of the partner in asking the
speaker to repeat key phrases involving emotional components
is also associated with co-counselling. Similarly the listener
can encourage the speaker to associate present unpleasant
thoughts and feelings with past happenings, so as to better
understand their meanings. This is important. People may need
time to discharge old pain that keeps them stuck in distorted
perceptions. Restructuring of these perceptions may not be
possible without the phase of insight that follows emotional
discharge.

Eventually, the whole group is brought together again and
anybody is invited to share their problem (not their partner's)
with the group as a whole. This may well lead to an individual
using the group as a vehicle for personal therapy. While this
is fine, particularly for members whose pathology is that they
always put themselves down for the good of the group, the
leaders must recognise that such a development has to be consistent with the needs of the group as a whole. The contract
is to participate in a workshop on coping with stress rather
than to participate in a therapeutic or for that matter an
encounter group.

This activity may well take the whole of session two (the
afternoon) particularly if personal therapy is involved. It is
likely to generate a lot of emotional energy, and at the end of
it some form of tension release exercise is desirable. If sufficient time remains a number of choices are possible. One is to
provide an opportunity for an individual who has made an offer
to demonstrate that offer to the group. Our experience is that
offers frequently lie within the area of body work; yoga,
masssage, or breathing relaxation. If the group is willing (and
suitably attired), such activities seem to provide a relaxing
passage through which to bring the session to a conclusion.
Indeed, were no offers to materialise, we would suggest that
simple massage of head and shoulders (and perhaps of arms and
legs) between couples is a highly suitable activity which re-
invests attention into the body and sponsors peaceful and
gentle emotions. It produces a quiet but warm ending to the
first day, which is half way through the workshop.

Other options
The process of working in pairs which is fostered in the cognitive restructuring work allows an opportunity to develop

further the idea of co-counselling. Apart from offering a useful series of techniques for stress management, it focuses on the role of helper and of being an active listener, albeit within a particular theoretical framework. Moreover, like massage it moves the agenda forward from cognition, into mobilising body energy and discharging painful emotions. A more totally alternative focus to session two which we have found to work well is one which concentrates on transactional analysis. If this pathway is followed, we have found it useful to present to participants a discussion of the three life scripts of Rescuer, Persecutor, and Victim. We then ask participants to complete a chart with Thinking, Feeling and Behaviour along the vertical axis, and Rescuer, Persecutor and Victim along the horizontal. The type of result this produces is shown in figure 4. The contents of each box are descriptions of each life script in the three forms of expression.

Figure 4: Life scripts and their thinking, feeling and behavioural expressions

|  | Rescuer | Persecutor | Victim |
|---|---|---|---|
| Thinking | Positive | Superior Dominant | Muddled |
| Feeling | Altruistic Smug Protective | Aggressive | Resentful Self pitying |
| Behaviour | Listening Peace-maker | Physically and verbally abusive | Refuse to accept responsibility for self Helpless |

Participants can also be asked to identify individuals they know in terms of these life scripts. They are encouraged to examine their own stresses, relating them to the extent to which they play one or more of these roles in particular situations and how they think feel and behave when in these roles.
    Transactional analysis is probably best presented as a substitute for cognitive restructuring rather than as additional to it. Both necessitate a certain amount of theoretical explication and taken together the two probably provide a slightly heavy menu for one session; included in separate sessions they might overbalance a workshop of the kind we are

Coping with Stress : A Framework for a Workshop

outlining in this paper. In diagrammatic form, therefore, the
second session may look something like as follows:-

| | | |
|---|---|---|
| Cognitive Re-structuring | ──────────────> | Body Work |
| or | | |
| Cognitive Re-structuring | → Co-counselling → | Body Work |
| or | | |
| Transactional Analysis | ──────────────> | Body Work |
| or | | |
| Transactional Analysis | → Co-counselling → | Body Work |

It goes without saying that no technique in a stress reduction
workshop should be used without sensitivity on the part of the
leaders. It is all too easy to employ methodologies like cognitive restructuring or transactional analysis which provide a
cognitive structure to explain events, in ways which diminish
rather than enhance the experience of the participants. This is
not a question of lack of goodwill or caring on the part of
group leaders, but rather a reference to the infinite complexity of human beings. It follows that this is not to be regarded as a rigid scheme but as an outline plan. It may well be
that the nature of a group necessitates time being spent on
rather different approaches to stress coping. Perhaps
physical and body work and relaxation training need to be
elevated in importance. This is the kind of question the
leaders must continue to ask. There are also a number of prog-
ressive relaxation training techniques available, some of which
employ in-vivo application involving the principles of desens-
itisation (see Wolpe and Lazarus 1966). In some situations, with
some people, and with some groups this may prove to be more
appropriate than, for example, transactional analysis.

Session 3
After warm-up exercises (the importance of which cannot be
sufficiently stressed), we have found it useful to develop the
third session by introducing the idea of on the one hand lack
of assertiveness and on the other hand aggression as sources of
stress. Assertiveness training is then presented offering useful insights and even skills in coping with situations in a
less passive, more assertive fashion but without being aggressive. While the latter involves expression achieved at the
expense of others, assertiveness involves emotional honesty
and expression whilst at the same time respecting the position
of others. Whereas aggression implies self-righteousness and
feelings of superiority, assertiveness is characterised by self
confidence accompanied by respect for the rights of others.
While the line between the two is often easier to draw in
theory than in practice, assertiveness can reduce internal
conflicts and tensions and lead to more effective ways of
coping with stress.
    The idea of assertiveness assumes that each person has a

33

number of rights, including the expectation of respect from
other people, to articulate his or her feelings and needs, to
express his or her own opinions, and to decide whether or not
to meet the expectations of others. In the words of the title
of a well-known book on the subject, lack of assertiveness is
characterised by the fact that 'when I say no, I feel guilty'
(Smith 1975). It is not our purpose in this chapter to provide
a detailed account of specific techniques (see Alberti and
Emmons 1974 and Osborn and Harris 1975) but rather to indicate
a few approaches which may be helpful in developing assertiveness as a coping skill. Assertiveness can be defined as concerned with the expression of personal rights and feelings and is
valuable because it encourages people to challenge the notion
that their behaviour results inevitably from their personality
traits. The idea that we need to learn ways of standing up for
our rights without violating the rights of others inevitably
produces positive reactions from participants who seem to recognise instinctively the way in which lack of assertiveness
produces stress. When asked to identify such situations they
mention areas like the difficulty in protesting to a shop about
a faulty consumer good; challenging unjustified criticism from
their superiors; or saying no to a request to take on unwanted
additional work or for a date they do not really desire.

There are a number of ways of developing the use of the
technique in coping with stress, but our experience has been
that the best policy is to get into role play as quickly as
possible. As a first step individuals can be asked to note down
the salient characteristics of situations in which they experience stress. Once again, emphasis is put upon the identification of thinking, feeling and body states. The leaders then
ask for volunteers willing to discuss their response with the
group as a whole. After a situation has been described, the
leaders encourage role play of the situation concerned. Any one
situation may involve a number of role plays. For example, let
us take the typical situation of the person who finds it
difficult to return a faulty good to a shop because they feel
vulnerable, open to attack, open to ridicule, frightened of
rejection etc. The role play may proceed something like this:

1. Subject plays customer. Another member plays shop
   keeper or assistant. Group observes role play. Participants are asked how it feels to be in the part? Was
   behaviour of the other person as expected? How did the
   behaviour of the subject influence the result of the
   interaction? Group members are then invited to comment
   on the interaction they have witnessed.
2. Roles are reversed. Subject plays shopkeeper/assistant.
   The customer role is played by either the same person
   in the previous role play or another participant or
   perhaps by a leader. The same process is undergone.
3. Depending on the progress being made, variations on the

theme can be engaged in. For example, the subject or
the other person can be asked by the leader to be
aggressive or passive or assertive in order to offer an
experience of what it is like to be in such a
transaction.

4. The process may well develop into the Gestalt technique
of the 'hot seat', in which the subject himself or herself engages in a debate between internal parts of self,
e.g. the part that says 'it's O.K. to complain' and the
part that says 'if I do I will look foolish'. The hope
is that this will facilitate the process of integration
of these parts, some of which may well be subconscious-
ly disowned. Note that Gestalt work is very powerful
and needs to be used with care.

A number of such role plays can be developed and gradually the
leaders can choose to introduce a number of skills which are
helpful in increasing assertiveness. Of these the best known is
'broken record', i.e. simply repeating one's demand in a clear,
unequivocal way without being diverted by an irrelevant or
manipulative response. There are other techniques useful in
such areas as disarming anger.

The value of monodrama (via using the 'hot seat' method)
has been referred to above. We have found that as we have
developed our work in the area of assertiveness, individual
participants have come to use this method as a source of
personal therapy, facilited by the fact that the method has
developed in a naturalistic fashion from the role play. In
particular, painful feelings about bereavement and relationship
with a deceased person have proved amenable to this approach.
Regret over messages left unsaid can be released. It seems to
offer a framework in which old tapes can be replayed and
emotional discharge can take place.

If sufficient time exists before lunch, a brief guided
fantasy may be offered in which participants are encouraged to
focus on visual images of stress. They are then asked, however
poor their degree of artistic skills, to draw these images on
large sheets of paper (one for each person). This usually
produces much interesting material for group discussions
through interpretation of drawings. Individuals often report
insights of which previously they were only dimly aware. The
activity is useful in developing the point that images or
models or ideas are often difficult to communicate in words and
that language is an obfuscator of emotions as well as a medium
of communication. At one workshop, a participant had made small
tears all round the edge of her paper. That, she said is how I
feel when stressed: 'frayed round the edges'. At the end of
this activity, the third session can be drawn to a close, and
lunch taken. Diagrammatically, therefore, session three looks
something like this.

Assertiveness Therapy   if time
        ↓          permits  Guided Fantasy → Visual Imagery
     Role Play
        ↓
Monodrama (Hot-Seat/Gestalt)

## Session 4

As we move into the fourth and final session, the need for
spontaneity becomes more and more important on the part of the
leaders. They must be sensitive to unmet needs within the
group and must structure the final session accordingly. The
content of this session will depend upon the analysis made over
lunch, but in practice often begins with some form of relaxation exercises, thus emphasising once again the body, mind,
emotions link. This may be continued with a guided fantasy if
this has not already taken place in the previous session. It
can be followed by an open encounter session which allows
individuals further opportunity for personal therapy or by
encounter games which encourage togetherness, increase spontaneity, making having fun acceptable and reproduce in symbolic
form many of life's problems in areas like communication and
decision making. Dynamic meditation (of which tapes are available on the open market) is another possibility which involves
some very active physical activity as a vehicle for bypassing
cognitive processes. Alternatively, a lot of the methodology
developed in the workshop can be drawn together through a more
integrated practice of co-counselling, if this has not already
been done sufficiently in session two. The point is that the
leaders have many options. What they do at this stage is a
function of their understanding of themselves and the group and
of the skills they possess. Following a similar pattern to that
used above, we may, therefore, represent session four diagram-
atically as follows:-

Relaxation Exercises → Dynamic Meditation
Relaxation Exercises → Open Encounter Session

As the workshop draws towards its end, we always offer some
time for the group to get together as a whole to engage in a
process of quiet reflection. This provides an opportunity for
participants to complete any unfinished business and for the
leaders to ask group members for feedback about the workshop.
Our experience is that this form of evaluation has been at
least as valuable as the more systematic questionnaire type of
enquiry, which we have also employed.

## CONCLUSION

There is always a risk in a venture of the kind described in
this chapter that through a process of post-facto logic, a
series of activities that have little connection can be

presented as a coherent and integrated process. We do not
pretend that the model we have evolved is one we sat down and
created from scratch. Indeed, to declare this would be to deny
what we believe is the primary strength of our workshop, which
is that it has evolved and developed as the direct result of
the accumulation of experience upon which we have reflected and
analysed. This has enabled us to refine our theories in such a
way as to reflect back upon practice, thus creating a meaningful praxis between theory and practice. We believe that the
result is an experience which makes sense in terms of theories
of stress management and coping strategies, but which is flexible enough to take account of the needs of individual participants and of the nature of each group. We do not claim that
the form we have created is the only model for this form of
workshop or that it cannot be improved, and indeed effective
evaluation is a subject on which we need to do further work.
However, we do believe that what we have constructed achieves
the objectives which it has set itself.

Finally, as we have emphasised that development and change
is a primary feature of the workshops, it is appropriate to
raise the question, how are they likely to develop in the
future? The answer is that while we remain eclectic, we have
increasingly come to favour the multi-modal approach pioneered
by Lazarus. The path forward seems likely to take us further in
this direction.

NOTES

1. This chapter is a revised and expanded version of a
paper entitled 'Coping With Stress : a Workshop Framework'
published in The British Journal of Guidance and Counselling
12,2, July 1984, pp. 141-153. Material from that paper is
published here with the kind permission of the Editors of that
journal.

2. One of the workshops has been filmed for a programme
entitled 'Learning in Groups' for an Open University course
(E355 'The Education of Adults'). It can be viewed on BBC 2 or
is available for purchase from Open University Educational
Enterprises.

REFERENCES

Alberti, R.E. and Emmons, M.L. (1974) Your Perfect Right - A
    Guide to Assertive Behaviour, Impact Press, U.S.A.
Beck, A.T. (1971) 'Cognition, Affect and Psychopathology',
    Archives of General Psychiatry, 24, pp. 495-500
Bond, M. and Kilty, J. (1982) Practical Methods of Dealing With
    Stress, Human Potential Research Project, University of
    Surrey (Mimeo), Guildford
Caplan, G. (1964) Principles of Preventive Psychiatry,
    Tavistock, London

Caplan, G. (1968) An Approach to Community Mental Health, Grune
    Stratton, New York
Davis, M., Eshelman, E.R. and McKay, M. (1980) The Relaxation
    and Stress Reduction Workbook, New Harbinger Publications
    Richmond CA
Dryden, W. (1984) 'Issues in the Eclectic Practice of
    Individual Therapy', in Ed. Dryden W. Individual Therapy
    in Britain, Harper and Row, London, p. 345
Holmes, T.H. and Rahe, R.H. (1967) 'The Social Readjustment
    Rating Scale', Journal of Psychosomatic Research, 11,
    pp. 213-218
Lazarus, R. (1978) The Stress and Coping Paradigm, University
    of California (Mimeo), Berkeley
Lazarus, A. (1981) The Practice of Multi-Modal Therapy
    McGraw-Hill, New York
Lazarus, R. and Launier R. (1981) 'Stress related transaction
    between person and environment' in Pervin, L.A. and
    Lewis, M. (eds) Perspectives in Interaction Psychology,
    Plenum Press, New York
Murgatroyd, S. (1981) 'Reversal Theory : a New Perspective in
    Crisis Counselling' British Journal of Guidance and
    Counselling, 9, 2, pp. 180-193
Murgatroyd, S. and Apter, M.J. (1984) 'Eclectic Psychotherapy :
    A Structural-Phenomenological Approach', in Ed. Dryden W.
    Individual Therapy in Britain, Harper and Row, London
    pp. 389-414
Murgatroyd, S. and Woolfe, R. (1982) Coping With Crisis :
    understanding and helping people in need, Harper and Row,
    London
Osborn, S.M. and Harris, G.G. (1975) Assertive Training for
    Women, Charles Thomas, Springfield, Ill
Pearlin, L.I. and Schooler, C. (1978) 'The Structure of Coping'
    Journal of Health and Social Behaviour, 19, pp.2-21
Smith, M.J. (1975) When I say no, I feel guilty, Dial Press,
    New York
Wolpe, J. and Lazarus, A.A. (1966) Behaviour Therapy Techniques,
    Pergamon, New York

Chapter Three

STRESS AT WORK : A WORKSHOP

STEPHEN MURGATROYD

INTRODUCTION

A previous chapter (see Chapter 2) outlined a workshop programme examining stress and coping for members of the public.
That programme, in which the author has actively participated
for over five years, makes two assumptions: 1. that the experience of stress upon which the workshop is focused is generalised rather than particular or individualised; and 2. that
the coping strategies with which it is concerned relate to
individual participants. In the workshop to be outlined here,
these assumptions are made: 1. that the stress upon which
this workshop is focused is related specifically to the
experience of work; 2. that the sources of stress are just as
likely to reside in the way in which work is organised as 'in'
the thoughts, feelings and behaviour of the person who is 'at'
work; 3. that the coping strategies which the workshop seeks to
examine are concerned with both the individual as worker and
with the organisation of that individual's work; and 4. the
workshop is therefore as much about organisational change and
development as it is about stress management for individuals.
    The workshops described here have been offered over the
last four years to a variety of professional and other groups.
These have included: 1. headteachers, their deputies and other
teachers attending management training programmes; 2. police
officers; 3. probation service workers; 4. nurses and hospital
managers; 5. health visitors; and 6. the employees of medium
sized companies undergoing change. Though most of this work
has been undertaken for public service organisations, the
workshops can be readily adapted to suit the specific organisation for which it is intended.
    In all cases, the workshop has been preceded by a period of
observation by the facilitator. This observation period is
intended to produce 'real-life' examples of stress behaviour
from within the organisation for which the workshop is intended
whilst at the same time enabling the leader to make concrete
the examples which he or she wishes to use. In addition, this

period of observation provides an opportunity for the individuals who are to subsequently attend the workshop to make known some 'stress points' to the leader.

The workshops have varied from between one and three days and have all taken place during normal working time. The number of participants has varied from a group of twelve (in the case of the probation service workers) to a group of twenty five (in the case of nurses and health authority managers). All have operated with one leader.

In this chapter, the basic assumptions of the workshop are examined and the workshop is described. Some specific examples are provided of the stress and coping materials which emerge and a series of issues which the leader has invariably needed to address are discussed.

STRESS AT WORK - THE BACKGROUND

The experience of stress at work is commonplace. For example, in studies of teacher stress up to one third of the teachers in medium sized mixed comprehensive schools have been found to be experiencing high levels of stress (Kyriacou 1980). Office of Health Economics statistics show that stress related illnesses are the major reasons for short-term sickness absence from work - accounting for over 40 million days in 1973 and increasing annually (Cooper 1981). Stress related work absence is a more severe problem than either days lost through industrial injury (Taylor 1974) or days lost through strike action in a normal year (Gillespie 1974).

The experiences of stress at work vary. Those that are mentioned often are:
1.  Difficulty in thinking rationally and seeing a problem sharply from a number of viewpoints;
2.  Rigidity of views and extended prejudice;
3.  Out of place aggression, hostility and cynicism;
4.  Withdrawal from relationships;
5.  Excessive smoking or drinking, unwanted sexual advances;
6.  The inability to relax, over-tiredness, impatience.

A thoroughgoing review of these stress reactions is provided by Holt (1982), Chernis (1980) and Cooper and Marshall (1980).

Holt (1982) also provides a detailed statement of the sources of stress at work which have been the subject of empirical study. These include:-
Time Variables
* non-standard working hours
* deadlines
* unreasonable time demands
Social and Organisational Properties of the Work Setting
* the pacing of machines
* organisational irrationality (red tape)

40

* work-load and overload
* responsibility load
* monotony
* over-participation
* poor labour-management relationships
Changes in Job
* loss of job or the fear of job loss
* demotion
* over-promotion
* lack of promotion
Role Related
* role stress and role conflict
* degree of control over work processes
* feedback and communication problems
Other Sources
* job complexity
* relationships with superiors
* degree of connectedness to others at work
* inequality or inadequacy of pay
* quantity-quality conflicts

Each of the topics mentioned in this listing are associated with at least one and often more research papers. This list, and more extensive versions of such a list, provide a useful starting point for thinking about the issue of stress at work as a topic for group experiential learning. This list can be useful for initial observations and discussions in a particular organisation.

What is also useful is to examine the kinds of variables which have been studied as 'moderating' the effects of work stress. These include: the stage of life a person has reached (Kellam 1974); the extent to which the person is a 'lark' or an 'owl' - more accurately, the capacity for wakefulness (Ostberg 1973); organisational attachment (Porter and Dubin 1975); Type A and Type B behaviour (Price 1982); Machiavellianism (Gemmill and Heisler 1972); group cohesiveness (Beehr 1976); social support within and beyond the workplace (Lieberman 1982); and organisational climate and structure (Argyris 1973; James and Jones 1974).

In looking at such listings, group leaders need to remind themselves of the complexity of work as a social and personal experience. Most workers have ambiguous feelings about both their own work and their place of work. Work stress is not easily divorced from stress in other areas of a person's life. Though it may be exacerbated or caused directly by some organisational feature, work may be inherently stressful because of the impact the need to labour has upon the way in which people think and feel (Leonard 1984) - the capacity of people to reduce work stress may thus be limited by the importance which work has in the lives of workers.

This last point essentially concerns the relationship

between the individual as a worker and the worker as an expression of an organisational 'system'. Experience of running and
designing these workshops for specific organisations suggests
that the group leader needs to have some understanding of what
kind of organisational system they are working in.

ORGANISATIONAL 'FAMILY' SYSTEMS AND STRESS

In designing a workshop for a specific organisation (i.e. a
particular group of nursing staff working on one ward, a city's
probation service or a specific school's staff), the group
leader needs to have an understanding of that organisation as
a system. A failure to achieve this will result (experience
suggests) in the workshop focusing upon individuals as either
the source or carriers of stress. One major purpose of the pre-
group observation period is to examine the organisation as a
system.
      There are a great many models a leader can choose to work
with. In selecting one (or some combination of models), the
leader should remember that the reason for choosing a model is
to provide a specific framework from within which workshop
participants can better understand their own organisation. The
model is a device to promote organisational development - a
process described more fully by Beckhard (1959), Bennis (1963,
1966) and Schein and Bennis (1965). In one sense it does not
matter which model is chosen as long as it is well understood
by the leader and has utility in providing participants with a
conceptual framework and a common language which they can use
to analyse their organisation and their place within it.
      In preparing the workshops described here it might be use-
ful to regard organisations as having similar properties to
those of families seeking to overcome some specific distress
through family therapy. In particular, the model of families as
systems, derived from the work of Salvador Minuchin and others
(Minuchin 1976; Minuchin and Fishman 1981) has been found to
have special value.
      According to this model, families and in this context
organisations, can be understood as systems by reference to
two dimensions. These are: 1. the extent to which those who are
members of the family or organisation feel that they relate to
each other; and 2. the capacity of the family or organisation
to cope with challenge or change. This model, elaborated by
Olson, Sprenkle and Olson (1979), envisages that these two
dimensions can be represented as each having four points:-

      Relationships: enmeshed; connected; separated; disengaged.
      Adaptability : chaotic; flexible; standard; rigid.

Elaborating these two dimensions, Murgatroyd et al. (1985)
describe them as follows. In terms of relationships: 1. enmeshed
- in which organisational members think, act and feel as one

unit; 2. connected - in which the organisation is a unit which
nonetheless derives strength from the individual contributions
of its members; 3. separated - the organisation is essentially
the sum of the individuals which comprise it; and 4. disengaged
- in which the organisation is essentially a unit of independ-
ent persons with few personal or social ties. As is clear from
these descriptions, this dimension concerns the extent to which
people see their activities as arising out of their relationship with others. In terms of adaptability: 1. chaotic - the
organisation responds to the need to change or react to
challenge in a disorganised and fruitless way; 2. flexibility
- the organisation responds with imagination and flexibility to
challenge or change, reviewing decisions and adapting to circumstances in a pragmatic way; 3. standard - the organisation
has a number of standard responses to challenges or change
which it calls upon in some sequential way; and 4. rigid - the
organisation has one response to challenge or change (e.g.
denial) which it always calls upon, irrespective of the challenge. This dimension is essentially about the level of responsiveness to change which the organisation has.

This model arises from the combination of these two dimensions in the form of figure 5 below. As can be seen, the model
presents a sixteen category description of organisations which
is useful in 'diagnosing' stress. In particular, the categories
represented by shaded areas in figure 5 are thought to be most
likely to promote what might be called systems stress.

Figure 5: A model Of organisation

| | Chaotic | Flexible | Standard | Rigid |
|---|---|---|---|---|
| Enmeshed | | | | |
| Connected | | | | |
| Separated | | | | |
| Disengaged | | | | |

Clearly, the ability of the group leader to objectively examine
the extent of 'systems stress' in the terms of this model is
directly related to the amount of time they are able to observe
the organisation and the kind of access they are given to those
within the organisation with whom they are subsequently to work.
In practice, it has been found helpful to briefly explain this
model to several of those who are to participate in the workshop and to ask them to indicate which of the sixteen 'cells'
in figure 5 best represents their own view of the organisation.
Leaders need to note that perceptions of the organisation
differ with status, so that some in senior management tend to
regard the organisation as 'flexible/connected' whilst those
at a lower level within the organisation regard the organisation as 'disengaged/chaotic'. This is in itself an interesting
starting point for the period of observation. The point to note
is that the design of a workshop that is organisation specific
needs to take into account the perception of the organisation
as a system, since these perceptions may of themselves give
rise to stresses at work.

The model is elaborated here because it is the model
found most useful. It is not the only model and may be too
abstract for some groups. Leaders need to locate a model of an
organisation that is appropriate to the group with whom they
are working and which has value to the workshop they are
offering.

SETTING UP THE WORKSHOP

There are a number of issues which need to be clarified before
the workshop can take place. The first concerns the question
'who is the client?'.

One view some organisations have taken when approaching
the author to offer a stress workshop can be summarised in
this way: 1. organisational stress exists here and is a problem for management - it impairs efficiency and creates an
unnecessary barrier to change; 2. management, in co-operation
with staff, therefore wish to examine stress in the organisation; 3. the purpose of such an examination is to reduce stress
so that the tasks determined by management can be better
achieved; and 4. therefore the client is management.

An alternative view is as follows: 1. organisational
stress exists and presents one problem for management and
another for those experiencing stress; 2. a workshop in which
work stress is explored honestly and genuinely is likely to
involve the exploration of conflicts between different interests within the organisation as well as ways in which individuals contribute to their own stress by the way in which they
view the organisation; and 3. therefore the clients can be
defined as the different interest groups which emerge during
the course of the workshop.

It is important that the leader is clear about which of

these two views he or she is working to, since they are likely
to produce different 'outcomes' from a management point of
view. The first, if adopted and successful, could increase the
extent to which management objectives are fulfilled. The
second, if pursued thoroughly, could lead to management being
asked to rethink both what objectives they pursue and how they
intend to pursue them, whilst at the same time exploring the
way in which individuals cope with stress.

This issue is essentially about consultancy. Is the group
leader working here exclusively for management or for that
group of people who participate in the workshop? The view
generally taken by the author in his practice is that the
latter group is the client group.

A second question that arises in the setting-up of such a
group concerns the rules of self-disclosure. It is not difficult to imagine that a stress group within an organisation can
be stressful to those who are not members of the group.
Questions such as 'I wonder who they're crucifying now...?' or
statements such as 'I don't want them dumping their stress on
me!' or concerns that 'things said in confidence to a member
of the stress group might be used in the group against me
when I'm not there to defend myself'...have all been heard in
conversation about such groups within an organisation. The
group leader needs to make sure that: 1. those within the
group are clear that all that is said or done in the group is
confidential; 2. that talk about persons who are not members of
the group should be restricted to statements of fact; and
3. that all members of the organisation should have a precise
and clear statement about what the group is and what it is
doing. These points are best conveyed in writing or through a
general meeting of all staff.

This leads to a third point: who should be there? In one
organisation the suggestion was made that only officers of a
certain grade should be 'permitted' to attend such a workshop.
It was pointed out both by several such officers and the group
leader that this group was just one 'stressed' group within
the organisation and that other groups (most notably, secretarial and clerical staff and middle management) appeared to be
experiencing a great deal of self-reported stress and should,
therefore, be allowed to attend the workshop if they so wished.
Senior management responded to this suggestion by drafting a
memo to all staff essentially stating that it was 'not appropp-
riate' for junior grade staff to experience stress, since their
work was relatively less important than that of the officer
grades in question. This draft memo (which was never sent out)
was used as an example of the stress to which such 'junior'
(sic) staff were subjected to by senior management and lead to
all categories of staff being able to volunteer to attend the
workshop.

The final point concerns the follow-up contract agreed by
the group leader. Experience suggests that workshop

participants need to know before the group commences what
follow-up is possible from the group leader. In particular,
they wish to know: 1. what individual support is available to
them after the group ends; 2. what action the group leader
(together with others from the group) might take if the group
seeks to change some organisational processes; and 3. whether
a subsequent meeting of the group facilitated by the group
leader will be possible so that progress in stress-reduction
can be reviewed. Such contracts as are possible will vary from
organisation to organisation. What is important is that the
group are aware of the status of follow-up possibilities at the
start of the workshop and that these follow-ups are explicitly
contracted for.

A THREE-DAY WORKSHOP

Much of the remainder of this chapter describes the running of
the three-day workshop on 'Stress at THIS Workplace'. The most
extensive workshop is described so that those seeking to offer
their own workshops may adapt and modify this design. Examples
are given throughout of responses to the activities suggested
and the group leader's decision making assumptions are examined
where appropriate.
    It has not been suggested that this design is the most
satisfactory or the most extensive. Rather, this design is
presented as a statement of the author's current workshop format which is being adapted and modified all the time. Nor is it
being suggested that this design is 'original' or especially
unusual. Rather, the design is being used to explore some of
the training issues that arise during the course of such a
workshop.

Day One
All workshops need to begin. Most workshops begin plainly and
simply. The tone of the first part of a workshop is most
frequently set by its first hour.
    What makes running a workshop in a specific organisation
difficult is that many participants in the group (and sometimes
all) know each other well and have relationships both at work
and beyond which make them very familiar with each other's
habits, likes, dislikes and concerns. It is the leader who
needs to be introduced to the group rather than the group being
introduced to each other by the leader. However, the leader has
a task of exploring the difference between the extent to which
participants think they know each other and the extent of their
actual knowledge. Introductory 'games' (Brandes and Phillips
1978; Brandes 1984) which seek to encourage disclosure about
feelings are especially helpful both in breaking ice and in
establishing the emotional climate of the group and its
members.
    Following a brief introduction to the themes of the

workshop, usually done in the form of a brief lecture, the
group is divided into smaller groups to perform a specific task
in which specific managerial and production roles are played.
Two such tasks have been especially useful: 1. the 'make a T-
shirt out of a newspaper, staples, sellotape and felt-tip pens
task' in which members play the roles of designer, cutter,
fitter, model and manager; or 2. the four letter word task, in
which groups of four people are given a dictionary and 100
letters on card (in 'Scrabble' order) and are then asked to
make as many four letter words as possible in two minutes -
production targets are then stepped up at 500% increments and
the group is observed to see how the group develops and uses
structure (full details are available in Woodcock 1979 at
p. 153).

There are two points to these kinds of exercise (other
examples are given in Woodcock 1979). First, they create a
team related climate through activities which are essentially
fun. Indeed, these activities are standard team building 'games'.
Second, these activities permit the group as a whole to examine
the stresses of role and production quickly. The production
task (T-shirt or four letter words) matters little; the fact of
a collaborative activity aimed at production is what matters.

Typical outcomes from these activities include these
points:

* when roles are adhered to rigidly, then task performance
  is impaired and role conflicts are observed;
* the absence of roles or structure also inhibits task
  performance and, though conflict is not always apparent,
  frustration becomes a source of stress in the group;
* some roles are experienced as inherently stressful, but
  for different reasons - for example, in the T-shirt
  task the model is often stressed because of boredom
  whilst the designer is often stressed because of inter-
  ference;
* stress is related to an understanding of the purpose of
  an activity - where a group can see no point to an
  activity they feel 'lost' or helpless and in turn experience stress.

These points are brought out in plenary discussion of the experience of the team task. Such discussions are particularly
helped if each of the task groups has been observed by a person
who has been briefed about typical stress points to look out
for.

This activity is then usefully followed by a number of
structured documentation tasks - identifying the nature of
stress as an experience, its sources at work and typical coping
strategies. The same procedures as outlined in the previous
chapter on stress workshops have been found to be most useful
and the same charts are used. The only difference is that
participants are asked to specifically look at the nature of

work-related stress. One reason why the charts described by
Woolfe are especially helpful is that they provide the individual with a way of documenting their experience of stress and
coping under a specific series of headings - thinking, feeling,
body and relationships with others. That is, the structured
documentation tasks encourage participants to think of stress
as an individual experience which he or she can document for
themselves.

Experience suggests that the discussion of the materials
produced during the small groups working on their documents
raises these kinds of points:
* to what extent is the experience of stress to do with
  personality?
* to what extent are the physical effects of stress harmful?
* how many of the sources of stress at work can be affected by an individual acting within the organisation?
* to what extent is stress (or, more accurately, arousal,
  necessary to performance at work?

These issues, which often arise during plenary discussions of
the materials generated in small groups can be answered or
examined in a variety of ways. In recent workshops we have used
the Type A Behaviour Scale given in Meichenbaum (1983) to explore the first point about personality. Type A behaviour is, in
a variety of American studies (but in only some British studies),
linked to coronary heart disease. This provides a useful starting point for the discussion of the relationship between stress,
behaviour and personality. In addition, the Type A behaviour
scale is also a reasonable description of the type of behaviour
which many feel they have to engage in if they wish to be
promoted within many organisations. This dual use has been
effective in promoting active and lively discussion of all the
points listed above and brings a degree of objectivity into
the discussion. (If it is used, participants should be made
aware that there is little British evidence linking Type A
behaviour to heart disease).

The question about the degree of arousal necessary to
perform certain tasks is also useful - participants can be
asked to list twenty activities they routinely undertake at
work without any kind of 'stress' (in the sense of arousal) at
all. They find this extremely difficult. In running these
groups over a number of years the highest number of work activities offered for this task has been eleven (e.g. writing letters on my own initiative; arranging lunches to thank people;
sorting my mail in the mornings; distributing newsletters and
useful information).

On completion of these tasks and the related discussion
it is helpful to introduce the model of an organisation described earlier explaining the two dimensions (relationships and
adaptability) and showing the sixteen category model. This is

not done in any elaborate or overly academic way - a brief
lecture of some 20-30 minutes is all that is needed. Participants are then asked to take the model home with them and perform two tasks: 1. locate the organisation for which they now
work in one of the sixteen cells of the model; and 2. give six
reasons why they think this 'box' is the right box for their
organisation. They are asked not to discuss this with others
attending the workshop either now or between the end of this
session and the beginning of the next.

This is a long and hectic day. Participants generally feel
tired at the end of the day - they have, after all, done most
of the work: the evidence of this is all around the room on
flip-charts and in materials generated during the activities.
The group leader needs to acknowledge this work and effort and
indicate to them the value it has throughout the day and at the
end of the day. In addition, the leader needs to take stock of
two kinds of information: 1. about the issues raised within the
group; and 2. about the relationships within the group. Listing
key points that need to be picked up and used the next day is
a useful exercise in ensuring that valuable points raised in
the first day are not lost. In addition, the drawing of socio-
grams of the participants can be helpful in identifying the
personal strengths and weaknesses of groups - it helps locate
the inter-personal dynamics of the group.

Day Two
Each day of the workshop needs to begin with some kind of team-
building activity intended to: 1. consolidate work completed
and 2. begin a new day in a spirit of mutual collaboration. A
brainstorming activity in three small groups around the topic:
'ways management create stress, sometimes without thinking
about it' is especially helpful. Whilst this, in some senses
repeats some of the work completed the day before, it is a
useful reinforcer of previous observations and provides a
direct link into the major work of the morning. It is helpful
to preface this brainstorming work with an ice-breaker activity.
Full details of brainstorming can be found in Hanks et al.
(1977).

The brainstorming produces varied responses in different
organisations. Common amongst them are these:

* by assuming a greater level of communication within
  the organisation than is in fact the case;
* by responding ad hoc to situations which require planned
  reactions;
* by exploiting personal relationships within the organisation in order to ensure the completion of a task;
* by having inner and outer groups for decision making
  with only the inner groups being privy to the full
  rationale for decisions made;
* by setting targets for production (or work loads) which
  are impractical and which it is known that they (the

managers) could not themselves cope with; and finally,
* by discouraging initiative and reducing the incentives
  for making suggestions for change and development.

These points are not always made so clearly, but they are often
evident in the points raised by groups of five or six who
brainstorm around this topic. They can be brought out in a
plenary discussion of the brainstormed lists. Whether or not
these specific points are made, it is useful to classify the
points made in terms of the two dimensions of the model -
relationships and adaptability - since this provides a link to
the 'homework' task and to the major activity to be undertaken
in the remainder of the morning session.

And then to the major activity. Having identified the
issues raised through the brainstorming and classified them in
terms of the model, the group is then split into pairs to
examine the results of their homework assignment - to position
their own organisation on the grid. The pairs are asked to
agree a contract and three contracts are available to them.
These are:

* Person x speaks and person y listens;
  person x asks person y just to listen and
  attend to what is said; then roles are reversed
  (the 'listen-to-me' contract).

* Person x speaks and person y listens;
  person x asks person y to question them for
  points of clarification or to improve understanding -
  person y is not to challenge, confront, disagree or
  otherwise reflect upon the points raised by person
  x; then roles are reversed (the 'question-me' contract).

* Person x speaks and person y listens;
  person x asks person y to be devil's advocate and
  to challenge and push them to be clear and to think
  through what has been said, even if person y agrees
  with all that person x says; then roles are reversed
  (the 'push me' contract).

The pairs are asked to discuss their homework for a fixed time
- either 20 or 30 minutes per person (40 or 60 minutes per
pair). The contracts are chosen freely from these three. For
many it is their first experience of setting a contract for
dialogue and they find this experience both interesting and
illuminating. Indeed, many report that it is the first time
they have felt actively listened to when offering their own
thoughts for some time. These contracts provide a valuable
learning point in themselves.

They are then asked to form groups of 6-8 and share their
experience of thinking about their organisation in this way.
Through this 'pyramiding' of experiences some disagreements
and issues begin to emerge about the organisation as an

organisation, thereby highlighting different perceptions of the organisation and suggesting different organisational stress experiences. Groups are asked to record on flip-chart paper the issues which they would like to raise in the full group meeting that is to follow. Some groups raise one or two issues, others a lot. What matters most about this session is that groups explore genuinely and openly their understanding and perceptions of the organisation's own dynamics. Experience shows clearly that this model is readily understood by participants in the workshops and is relevant and meaningful as a way of understanding what happens to them as organisational members. They can and do use it as a basis for structuring a great deal of experience.

All this is still being undertaken in small groups - the leader moving between them to help clarify tasks and to ensure recording. The major activity ends with all of the groups coming together and engaging in an encounter which seeks to share all that has been discussed with the leader acting as the 'conscience' of the group as much as possible. The word 'encounter' has been deliberately chosen, since it accurately reflects what it is that happens at this point. Participants disclose their inner-most feelings about their place as members of the organisation whilst at the same time they look at the organisation as an object.

This encounter is difficult for a number of reasons. The first is that the experiential grounding of participants in their organisation is more substantial than that of the leader. This leads to the organisation being examined at a variety of levels by participants, not all of which are readily available to the leader. This in turn puts some pressure on the leader to explore these levels without encouraging a flood of irrelevant anecdotes about the organisation. The second reason that this is a difficult session is that participants are generally not used to being so open about the organisation. Openness of this kind clearly carries dangers, especially since others present might subsequently pose 'threats' to the person who is disclosing. The leader needs to ensure both that the 'setting-up' contract is clear and that the contract is fresh in the minds of participants at the beginning of this encounter. The final reason that this is a difficult session is that it often involves painful disclosures. The leader has to work hard to ensure that this pain is not used to avoid key issues but is actually regarded as a necessary part of the learning process (Gray 1983). A general discussion of these forms of encounter can be found in Rogers (1979).

This encounter session needs time - experience suggests that it will run throughout the afternoon. The leader should ensure that all the relevant material generated by the processes used to create the encounter (i.e. homework, brainstorming, pyramiding, disclosure, contracting) are examined and acknowledged before the encounter is formally

ended. This requires the leader to check-out the thoughts and
feelings of participants and to exercise skilled judgement.

Before moving on to develop the activities for the remainder of the workshop, the leader generally needs to inject some
energy into the group. 'Mixed-Veg', described more fully in the
previous chapter on stress workshops, is especially valuable.
Whatever the 'game' chosen, it needs to involve the use of
physical activity and humour.

Day Three
At this point the workshop can take two directions. Either it
can choose to examine the way in which this group might seek
to affect the organisation so that 'it' is a less stressful
place to be; or it can choose to examine the extent to which
these individuals can seek to change themselves so that they
experience less stress within themselves when they are in the
organisation. The discussion of this decision needs to be open
and direct - it is not a decision that the leader takes on
their own initiative, since it is critical to the nature and
success of the workshop itself. The remainder of this chapter
assumes that the decision is made to pursue the organisational
option, since the personal option is examined in the chapter
by Woolfe earlier in this volume.

When this decision has been made the group needs to renew
its contract. The success of the group depends upon its understanding of the contracts it has and upon the ability of the
group to respect the rights and intentions of others. To some
extent, the ability of the group to be an organisation in its
own right provides the resources and incentives for the group
to change or seek to affect the organisation.

The remainder of the workshop is concerned with: 1. promoting relationship change within the organisation and 2. examining the ways in which the organisation can improve its
responsiveness to change, challenge or external threat. These
two territories of work (both of them can only be touched on
in the time remaining) occupy the remaining time of the workshop. In pursuing these two themes it is important to encourage
individuals within the groups to accept resonsibility for
their own part in the organisation - the organisation is in
part themselves.

RELATIONSHIPS

The focus of attention during the relationship development
phase of the workshop is upon basic communication skills. Some
of the language conventions used in gestalt work, described
more fully in Murgatroyd (1985) are used to teach participants
that relationship quality is very much a function of the
language used. In addition, some of the communication principles developed by Grinder and Bandler (1976) for dealing with
three common communication problems (over-generalisation,

systematic deletion and distortion) are also presented. It is
also necessary to structure some practice exercises which show
the way in which these communication problems arise and can be
dealt with.

Problems about relationships within an organisation are
more than problems of communication. By using communications as
a starting point, though, it is often possible to show both how
the relationship problem is communicated and what the person
can do about it. Sometimes, the problems of communication
relate to artificial boundaries created by the organisation
around specific members. For example, there is a problem about
communication between different status level members within the
organisation. It is important that the facilitator recognise
that these difficulties cannot be overcome by reference to
individual communication skills and understandings alone, but
that some organisational change may also be needed. Typically,
these changes involve separating out organisational function
(to which status is related) and the quality of relationship
between people within the organisation (which are not necessarily status bound). This subtle point - that there is a
difference between what people do and what people are - is
often difficult for individuals to grasp, but is important if
relationships are unduly affected by status concerns. Some 'of
the work developed within rational-emotive therapy about relationships (see Dryden 1984) is especially valuable here.

Throughout this period of work (which can last a half day
or more) it is important to utilise the communication skills
being promoted within the group itself. Thus the facilitator
needs to establish some basic communication rules for the
group's work. These include: 1. discourage 'why' questions and
encourage such questions to be converted into statements about
what happens or what is experienced and how this comes to
happen or be experienced; 2. encourage talk in the first person
and not in the third person - 'I' statements are preferable to
'it' statements since they encourage and enable a person to
more directly own their thoughts and feelings; 3. stop individuals broadcasting their thoughts and feelings as if they were
disc-jockeys on a local radio station - enable them to talk in
specific and exact terms about their thoughts and feelings and
encourage them to talk directly to the person or group whom
they feel should hear their message; 4. do not permit or
encourage the use of 'can't' statements (e.g. 'I can't possibly
say that to him') and instead require participants to say
'won't (e.g. 'I won't say that to him'), since this too encourages ownership of feelings, thoughts and actions; finally 5.
Discourage the use of questions and encourage the use of statements, since this also promotes ownership. These five language
devices are intended to encourage individuals to become more
direct in their statement of their own thoughts and feelings
and to become more assertive within the organisation.

A second feature of this period of work is a concern with

the purpose of communication and relationship within an organisation. For some reason, a great many individuals within an
organisation think and feel that the organisation should be
happy at all times, should be free from any organisational
stress or individual distress and should not experience difficulty. That is, the organisation should possess a consensus like
emotional quality and be consistent in its qualities. The
leader needs to examine the irrationality of these beliefs in
terms of the set of irrational beliefs outlined by Ellis (1962).
Of particular value is an exploration of these three irrational
beliefs: 1. 'that it is important to be loved by all those who
work in the organisation - if someone does not like you then
you must act to make them like you'; 2. 'you must be thoroughly competent and achieving at all times if you are to be loved
and respected within the organisation, a failure will lead
others to reject you as a person'; and 3. 'it is terrible when
things are not the way I would like them to be and I must work
hard to secure changes that make things the way I would like
them'. These three irrational beliefs, commonly understood by
workshop participants, usually act as a trigger for the
identification of other such beliefs. The leader needs to work
with the group as a whole to show the irrational nature of
these beliefs and to encourage a more rational statement of
their underlying features.

By linking communication skills, assertiveness and
rational thinking the leader is able to develop an active
programme of work for participants which seeks to develop their
own skills for building relationships whilst at the same time
locating changes that need to be made at an organisational
level to facilitate relationship enhancement. This session
normally ends with a group writing individual contracts about
changes in their relationships with others which they intend
to make and a group contract indicating organisational changes
which they would like to see implemented, so that relationship
building can be assisted rather than hindered by their
organisation.

The most substantial practical problem the leader needs
to deal with during this phase of the workshop is the refusal
to recognise that relationship difficulties stem from conjoint
failures in communication. Individuals tend to attribute blame
and this in itself obstructs constructive communication. The
leader needs to use any expression of blame or guilt as a
vehicle for looking at the failure of communication linked to
irrational beliefs.

ORGANISATIONAL CHANGE

When the group attends to the issue of enhancing the organisation's responsiveness to challenge, threat or change (usually
in the final afternoon) then the communication skills and
rules which have been developed in the previous session provide

valuable reminders of how open communication facilitates both connectedness and flexibility. The leader needs to begin this session with a reminder of the organisational model which forms a backdrop to the workshop (see figure 5) and the interaction between the nature of communications and relationships and the capacity to deal with change. A brief reminder session is usually needed to achieve this.

At one time at these workshops, participants were asked to use historical experiences of change to understand what was wrong with the organisation's response. This practice has been supplanted by asking the group to examine the idea of quality circles. In part this is because a lot of the material generated through historical reflection brought the group back to communication failure and in part because it forced the groups to deal with these issues only with the tools already available to them. This task aims to provide a resource for the group to develop insights into organisational processes and to encourage systematic and careful evaluation of options. Quality circles permit this.

The idea behind a quality circle is simple: a group of like-status people meet regularly (every two weeks, for example) to discuss the quality of the organisation's work (its atmosphere, its 'products', its current challenges, etc.) and try to identify actions which the circle's members can complete which would contribute to improving the quality of the organisation. The circle members can be from any level within the organisation and can be concerned with just one feature of it (e.g. the quality of staff relationships) or several. The point is that a meeting takes place and issues are discussed openly and with conviction with the intention that the expression of ideas and concerns will be carefully attended to by all other members and that some direct action outcomes will result. It is not intended that this circle should recommend action to others (i.e. senior management) unless it can be matched by some action initiative from within the circle. Quality circles are described more fully in Mohr and Mohr (1983).

To aid the idea of a quality circle meeting, the leader presents a simple device know as a STOP. This is an acronym for four headings which a quality circle will often use in brainstorming ideas and issues - strengths (what are the strengths of this organisation/suggestion/idea), threats (in what way does this development threaten others), opportunities (what opportunities would arise if we acted in the way suggested) and problems (what practical problems will arise in our attempts to implement this strategy or idea or suggestion). The idea is that a quality circle would take these headings and use a STOP as a basis for brainstorming around a specific issue within the organisation at this time.

What happens in the workshop is that the leader creates a quality circle by using the group to look at a specific issue and acting as a process consultant to the group. The task of the leader is to: 1. highlight communication issues within the group; 2. to encourage the correct use of brainstorming; 3. to show how a STOP analysis facilitates active problem solving and connectedness; and 4. to provide a vehicle from which participants can generalise from this specific experience to the potential of a quality circle within their organisation.

To make this procedure more concrete, here are the results of a particular group of workers brainstorming the problems associated with the introduction of new technology (the source of a lot of the identified stress in the organisation):

Strengths
* speeds information exchange within the unit
* ensures direct links between writers and printers
* lower costs
* shorter time between ideas and products
* equalising roles within the same status
  level of the organisation
* can be added to as technology develops
* shared skills
* recognition of the part played by others is more direct

Threats
* individuals are swamped by the new technology
* those who were highly regarded before find it
  difficult to master the new technology and find
  themselves held in lower esteem
* threatens support workers who no longer need to
  support others
* permits closer monitoring of staff than hitherto
* requires staff to constantly update their technical
  skills irrespective of their interests in doing so

Opportunities
* higher work rates
* more control over 'products' than before
* being able to collaborate with others without
  having to set up elaborate meetings - (a specific
  feature of the technology,

Problems
* not well understood
* poor selling of the idea
* difficult to get used to
* can't teach an old dog new tricks.

This is usually a powerful activity. It can be powerful when the issue to be addressed is discerned by the leader before the workshop begins. This is best achieved by seeking to identify the most pressing issue within the organisation and by

the leader seeking to anticipate what the STOP might look like
when completed. The leader should also remember that his or
her task is to act as a process consultant seeking to highlight
the way in which the circle is communicating and relating to
each other rather than seeking to add to the solution to the
organisational problem the group is looking at. The leader's
expertise is about <u>process</u> not about this organisation at this
time.

ENDING

This is long and complex workshop which covers many issues and
concerns. It is also usually highly emotional and charged with
anxiety about the link between participants and other organisational members. The leader needs to end by reinforcing several
points. Amongst them are these: 1. the contract the group has
about confidentiality; 2. the value of seeing organisational
problems as linked directly to the quality of relationships;
3. the need for increased flexibility in organisational
problem-solving to be matched by better connectedness within
the organisation; 4. the responsibility the individual has for
their own connectedness and the quality of their own relationships; and 5. the need for collectivity (through the quality
circle), for promoting flexibility and change.
    If the leader ended the session with a brief summarising
lecture they would not do justice to the quality of individual
learning which most often takes place when this workshop has
been offered. These workshops normally end with two specific
activities; 1. participants are asked to write a letter to
themselves which will be posted back to them in six months
time - the idea being that this letter will be a self-contract
committing them to some task; and 2. by trying to have some fun
usually through a game which shows the quality of relationships
within the group (see Brandes 1984).

REFLECTION

This is an emotionally demanding group for anyone to run, as
the description provided here shows. It is so demanding that
there are times when the leader is inclined to lose focus.
It might be helpful to carry a small card which simply reads
'I know too little about this organisation to seek to change
it', which acts as a reminder that the leader is an organisational development worker concerned with the process of communication and stress reduction. He or she does not carry execu-
tive responsibilities within the organisation.
    A second concern is that such a workshop can create
expectations amongst participants that the organisation will
be more responsive to their needs because (usually) the group
has become more responsive and sensitive to each other's needs
as the workshop progresses. The leader needs to ensure that the

group are aware of how their experience within the group is unique to them and how they will need to work at their own communications and relationships with others if they wish the work of the workshop to be translated in a useful way for others.

Finally, this particular stress workshop as a design is not necessarily the most effective use of the emotional energy available in the group. What is apparent is the utility of using a conceptual model of the organisation as a basis for linking concerns about relationships and change to stress. To some extent, all of these workshops validate this device as a learning vehicle for organisational members.

As yet only one follow-up study concerning the stress levels amongst workshop participants who have attended a workshop has been conducted. The eighteen individuals all reported that, after the workshop, they found stress less debilitating since they felt they better understood its origins and its effect as well as their own part in maintaining it. This same group had split into two quality circles which met fortnightly and found that they would spend some of the time at each meeting talking about stress felt by participants. In effect, the workshop had provided a basis for the creating of ongoing self-help groups. As for the flexibility of the organisation, they noted that little had changed, though some interest was now being shown in some of the ideas produced by the quality circle group in which one of the assistant managers was a participant.

How typical these reactions are it is not possible to say. It seems that these outcomes are the best that can be expected from a high level of emotional investment over an extremely short period of time.

## REFERENCES

Argyris, C. (1973) 'Personality and Organization Theory Revisited', Administrative Science Quarterly, Vol. 18, pp. 141-167

Beckhard, R. (1959) 'An Organizational Improvement Program in a Decentralized Organized Organization', in Zand, R. and Buchanan, D. (eds) Organizational Development - Theory and Practice, Academic Press, New York

Beehr, T.A. (1976) 'Perceived Situational Moderators of the Relationship Between Subjective Role Ambiguity and Role Strain', Journal of Applied Psychology, Vol. 61, pp. 35-40

Bennis, W.G. (1966) Changing Organizations, McGraw-Hill, New York

Bennis, W.G. (1963) 'A New Role for the Behavioural Sciences - Effecting Organizational Change', Administrative Science Quarterly, Vol. 8, pp. 125-165

Brandes, D. (1984) Gamesters Handbook Two, Hutchinson, London

Brandes, D. and Phillips, H. (1978) Gamesters Handbook, Hutchinson, London

Chernis, C. (1980) Staff Burn-Out-Job Stress in the Human
    Services, Sage, Beverly Hills
Cooper, C.L. (1981) The Stress Check - Coping with the Stresses
    of Life and Work, Prentice-Hall, Englewood, New Jersey
Cooper, C.L. and Marshall, J. (1980) White Collar and
    Professional Stress, John Wiley and Sons, New York
Dryden, W. (1984) Rational Emotive Therapy - Fundamentals and
    Innovations, Croom Helm, London
Ellis, A. (1962) Reason and Emotion in Psychotherapy, Lyle
    Stuart, Seacaucus, New Jersey
Gemmil, R. and Heisler, W.J. (1972) 'Machiavellianism as a
    Factor in Managerial Job Strain, Job Satisfaction and
    Upward Mobility', Academy of Management Journal, Vol 15,
    pp. 51-62
Gillespie, F. (1974) 'Stress Costs More than Strikes',
    Financial Times, 26 April
Gray, H.L. (1983) 'The Pain of Learning', European Journal of
    Humanistic Psychology, Self and Society, Vol 10(4),
    pp. 168-172
Grinder, J. and Bandler, R. (1976) The Structure of Magic
    (2 Vols), Science and Behaviour Books, Palo Alto,
    California
Hanks, L., Belliston, L. and Edwards, D. (-977) Design Yourself,
    William Kaufman, Los Altos, California
Holt, R.R. (1982) 'Occupational Stress', in Goldberger, L. and
    Breznitz, S. (eds), Handbook of Stress - Theoretical and
    Clinical Aspects, Free Press, New York
James, L.R. and Jones, A.P. (1974) 'Organizational Climate -
    A Review of Theory and Research', Psychological Bulletin,
    Vol 81, pp. 1096-1112
Kellam, S.G. (1974) 'Stressful Life Events and Illness', in
    Dohrenwend, B.S. and Dohrenwend, B.P. (eds), Stressful
    Life Events - Their Nature and their Effects, John Wiley,
    New York
Kyriacou, C. (1980) 'Occupational Stress Amongst School
    Teachers - A Research Report', Curriculum and
    Organizational Research in Education, Vol 4(3), pp. 86-122
Leiberman, M.A. (1982) 'The Effects of Social Supports on
    Responses to Stress', in Goldeberger, L. and Breznitz, S.
    (eds), Handbook of Stress - Theoretical and Clinical
    Aspects, Free Press, New York
Leonard, P. (1984) Personality and Ideology - Towards a
    Materialist Understanding of the Individual, Macmillan,
    London
Meichenbaum, D. (1983) Coping With Stress, Century, London
Minuchin, S. (1976) Families and Family Therapy, Tavistock,
    London
Minuchin, S. and Fishman, H.C. (1981) Family Therapy Techniques,
    Harvard University Press, Cambridge, Massachusetts
Mohr, W. and Mohr, H. (1983) Quality Circles - Changing the
    Image of People at Work, Addison-Wesley, New York

59

Murgatroyd, S. (1985) Counselling and Helping, British
    Psychological Society, Methuen, London
Murgatroyd, S., Cade, B. and Shooter M. (1985) 'Family
    Relationships and Counselling', British Journal of
    Guidance and Counselling, Vol 12(1), pp. 45-56
Ostberg, O. (1973) 'Interindividual Differences in Circadian
    Fatigue Patterns of Shift Workers', British Journal of
    Industrial Medicine, Vol 30, pp. 341-351
Porter, L.W. and Dubin, R. (1975) The Organization and the
    Person - Final Report of the Individual Occupational
    Linkages Project, Office of Naval Research, Washington,DC,
Price, P.A. (1982) Type A Behaviour Pattern - A Model for
    Research and Practice, Academic Press, New York
Rogers, C.R. (1979) On Encounter Groups, Penguin, Harmondsworth
Schein, E.G. and Bennis, W.G. (1965) Personal and
    Organizational Change Through Group Methods, John Wiley
    and Sons, New York
Sprenkle, D. and Olsen, D. (1978) 'Circumplex Model of
    Marital Systems - Empirical Studies of Clinic and Non-
    Clinic Couples', Journal of Marriage and Family
    Counselling, Vol 4, pp. 59-74
Taylor, R. (1974) 'Stress at Work', New Society, 17 October
Woodcock, M. (1979) Team Development Manual, Gower Press,
    Aldershot, Hampshire

Chapter Four

TRAINING IN BASIC COUNSELLING AND COMMUNICATION SKILLS :
A WORKSHOP FORMAT

TONY HOBBS

THE RELEVANCE OF BASIC COUNSELLING/COMMUNICATIONS SKILLS
WORKSHOPS

It is likely that a more active knowledge of the basic skills
involved in interpersonal communication would be of benefit to
very many people - not solely those engaged in attempting to
help others. Practising counsellors and psychotherapists daily
recognise the major role played by mis-communication, and the
lack of communication, in the development of their clients'
difficulties. This is apparent when working with individuals
and when working in a group setting, especially with couples
and families.

Possessing an increased understanding of basic counselling
and communication skills eases the difficulties which many
people have come to expect in their relationships with others.
Such changes come about through developing a person's ability
to receive more accurately messages from others and then to
be able to respond in a manner which lets them know they have
been understood. This helps people recognise they are being
carefully listened to and encourages them both to listen to
themselves more carefully and to say more. Nelson-Jones
described two people in a conversation as each waiting for an
opportunity to talk, 'to exercise their own egos', and so
focusing on themselves and their own thoughts rather than on
the other person and what he or she is saying. However, he
described the more counselling orientated encounter as where
the focus of the listener remains instead of fully on the speaker
(Nelson-Jones 1975). At appropriate moments the listener
checks out what they believe they have heard.

At a broader level, considerable benefits have already
been demonstrated in politically sensitive areas, situations
where interpersonal misunderstandings are rife, sometimes
dangerously so. Carl Rogers describes how providing experience
in a basic encounter group in Northern Ireland enabled groups
of Protestants and Catholics to come to appreciate just how
seriously they had misunderstood each other (Rogers 1978).

Participation in the encounter group, where emphasis was laid firmly on increasing the level of effective interpersonal communication, led directly to these few members of both religious groups actively recognising the manner in which their stereotyped prejudices affected not only their own day to day lives but also that of the cultures in which they lived. Indeed, nowadays Rogers invests a considerable proportion of his working time in running cross-cultural communication workshops designed to break down such barriers between representatives of different nations and cultures. He has recently commented on the important role which these communication workshops have to play (see Hobbs 1986).

The psychotherapy literature has repeatedly supported the value of these basic skills. They are seen as essential to the effective practice of person-centred therapy and development as a therapist (Rogers 1942, 1951 and 1961), and the humanist movement in psychotherapy has since largely adopted them as fundamental to its various approaches to therapy. There exists a variety of approaches to therapy (Parloff 1976; Goldfried 1980). Influential reviews (Luborsky, Singer and Luborsky 1975; Glass and Miller 1980) together with frequently cited studies (Sloane et al 1975) support the proposition that outcomes of these diverse therapies are similar. Such studies can be interpreted as lending support to the idea that an important determinant in the outcome of therapy is the proficiency of the therapist in basic skills. Some recent British research has shown that whilst therapists are often seemingly unaware of what their clients perceive as being helpful (Llewellyn and Hume 1979; Llewellyn 1984), patients who perceived the therapist as communicating warmth and genuineness, two of the central counselling skills, improved more than those patients who rated the therapist as being less warm and genuine in their manner. This was the case whatever was the 'objectively' measured outcome (Smail 1978).

## THE COUNSELLING/COMMUNICATION SKILLS

Counselling skills can be conceptualised as falling into three levels of degree of expertise, 'basic', 'intermediate' and 'advanced'. At the 'basic' level these skills are common with those fundamental to effective communication in general and it is with these that this chapter is concerned.

The skills at the most basic level are those of 'attentive' and 'active' listening (Ivey 1983):

1. Attending behaviour and provision of minimal encouragements to talk.
2. Use of 'open' and 'closed' questioning strategies.
3. Selective listening skills - paraphrasing and summarising.
4. Reflection of feelings.

From the outset it should be understood by each participant
that in practice all these skills, at whichever level, are not
techniques to be applied in a mechanistic manner, but instead
are simply skills which, when combined, form an effective way
of relating to others. Just as smooth and safe driving depends
on the driver having learnt to properly use the control pedals,
how to turn, reverse, speed up, slow down, use the mirror, etc.
and then to be able to combine each of these skills until their
integrated practice becomes practically second nature, so it is
with counselling skills.

At the 'intermediate' level the skills are more to do with
enhancing effective two-way communication with the client and
developing personal exploration. They include the four therapeutic conditions which form the core of Rogerian or person-
centred therapy, originated by Carl Rogers (Rogers 1942, 1951,
1957). Rogers himself has recently again emphasised the need to
guard carefully against the 'mechanistic' application of such
skills (Hobbs 1986). Although listed here both these and the
advanced counselling skills will only be briefly referred to
here as more detailed coverage lies outside the remit of this
chapter. They are:
  1. Therapeutic genuineness/congruence.
  2. Respect/unconditional positive regard.
  3. Empathic understanding.
  4. Concreteness/specificity.

There exist two major phases in the person-centred approach to
working with people therapeutically. The first is where the
therapist works to establish the safety of a therapeutic relationship between him or herself and the client, drawing on
skills at the basic and intermediate level. The second is one
where the therapist takes more of the initiative in the
sessions and works toward helping the client both make
decisions and act. In a sense the therapeutic conditions at the
'intermediate' and 'advanced' level are less skills that are
taught, but more ones that develop in the individual therapists
as a result of their own developing insight into the philosophy
of the 'model' in use.

The 'advanced' level skills are those termed to be 'action
orientated' therapeutic dimensions of person-centred therapy;
  1. Confrontation.
  2. Self disclosure.
  3. Immediacy.

The focus of the workshops described in this chapter is on
training in basic skills - possession of which is nevertheless
fundamental to effective development of a person's counselling
abilities. From the first moment of involvement the establishment of a therapeutic atmosphere will require the counsellor to
be able to draw on his or her capacity to operate at any of

these three 'levels'. It should therefore be recognised that it is not the intention of this chapter to be seen as providing a description of a complete counsellor training programme

## THE TRAINING WORKSHOPS

### The Micro-Counselling Skills Teaching Model

The training approach in these workshops is that of micro-counselling, as developed in the United States by Allen Ivey (Ivey 1968, 1971; Ivey and Authier, 1978; Ivey 1983). This approach has been the focus of extensive research over almost twenty years and is one of the few programmes to have been shown to be effective. The micro-counselling format focuses on the training of specific behavioural skills. From a research practitioner viewpoint, these behavioural skills are considerably easier to define and empirically demonstrate than are the comparatively less empirically observable variables of other approaches to counsellor training. It is also easier to assess their reliability. In over 150 research studies with trainees from various professional and non-professional backgrounds, there has now been practical validation of the effectiveness of this format of basic skills training in achieving training objectives (Kasdorf and Gustafsen 1978).

The micro-counselling model itself provides a flexible structure for experiential learning to take place and workshops are normally enjoyed by both participants and workshop organisers - although they demand hard work which is often personally challenging in nature. Time spent on didactic teaching is minimised; the trainees are encouraged to become more consciously aware of the skills which they already possess and to both develop and refine these skills further.

Micro-counselling teaching comprises five basic stages and teaching of each of the four basic skills (attending, questioning, paraphrasing, reflecting) is approached separately but in the same manner. After exercises to 'warm up' the group the first stage is for the participants to read a concise description of the specific skill to be focused upon. This is provided for them in the form of a handout by the workshop organiser. Adequate time is needed for reading and reflection.

The second stage is to provide a demonstration of the skill to be taught. Whether this is done by use of a pre-recorded video-tape or by live modelling by the workshop organiser or a colleague (together, or with the help of one of the workshop participants) is a matter of choice. Both methods have their strengths and weaknesses. A video recording will enable the quality and clarity of the interaction to be controlled and so guarantee a clear demonstration of the skill in question. However, such recordings are less personal than a live demonstration, the demonstrators cannot be asked questions about the events in the video (unless they are running the workshop) and video machinery may not be available for use in the

training workshops. Live demonstrations guarantee both a sense
of involvement for the observers and act as a model for breaking the ice in observers' own subsequent role plays in the
training sessions, as described below. However, it is not
possible to guarantee the quality of the relevant skill being
shown to the participants in a clear manner.

The third stage involves role play practice in threes of
the specific skill, each participant taking turns at role-
playing the counsellor, role-playing the client and acting as
careful observer of the interactions of the two role-players.
The fourth stage is one in which honest and constructive feedback is provided by participants and workshop organisers on
the content of the role-plays. After a period for questions
and discussion, the fifth and final stage begins. It involves
basically repeating the third stage of role-plays in threes,
this time with modifications suggested in the feedback session
being actively practised. This is then followed by a further
feedback session.

In real-life usage, each of the relatively distinct basic
skills taught by the use of this model will overlap considerably. It is useful to view these basic skills as a hierarchy; for
example, reflection of feeling building on the foundation of
attentive listening skills and the use of open questions.

The style of running these workshops described in this
chapter and based on this micro-counselling skills approach has
evolved over time and has been modified by experience. The
model has been found to be effective in teaching these basic
skills in workshops for clinical psychologists, counsellor
trainees, medical staff, physiotherapists, nurses and nurse
tutors, outpatients of a psychiatric hospital, lecturers in
higher education and many others.

Preparation
The following points may be useful in planning a workshop of
this kind.

Participants. Workshop leaders need to make decisions about
the number of participants in the workshop. There are certain
limiting factors, such as personal preference, the number of
co-workers available, size of room or rooms available and the
prior experience of workshop organisers. From experience, it
would seem advisable not to have more than fifteen trainees.
If there are more than nine persons (three groups of three) a
co-worker is desirable. The workshop described here uses triads
as the basis for training. It is possible, if really necessary,
to work in fours by having two persons acting as observers. It
is undesirable to discard the role of observer because in this
role important vicarious learning can take place. These training sessions provide very valuable opportunities to observe
what works for oneself and for others, in addition to recognising and considering both own and others' 'mistakes' and their

effects. It is better for participants to get it wrong in a workshop where the effects can be examined and participants can learn immediately from constructive feedback.

Few participants have come across the micro-counselling teaching model prior to the workshops. It can, therefore, be beneficial to prepare participants by informing them that they will be taking part in an experiential workshop in which they will be encouraged to assess their own skills and provide feedback on the skills of other members of the group. It is also useful to suggest to people that they might like to record themselves 'interviewing' a friend or other person for about fifteen minutes on whatever topic he or she might choose. This tape can later provide an interesting personal record for participants and act as a yardstick against which to measure their later development.

The physical setting. The physical setting affects the developing group atmosphere. As far as possible, the room in which the workshop is held should be warm and ventilated, comfortable, informal, private and free from external interruptions and noise. Ideally, a selection of rooms should be available. One of these should be large enough for whole group discussions and demonstrations, while smaller other rooms could be used by the triads for role-plays. In order to encourage participants to relax, seating arrangements should be as informal as possible and some form of refreshment could be available prior to the beginning of the session.

A portable video system is helpful in providing immediate, accurate feedback on someone's performance. It can be an effective way of enabling self-appraisal in the light of comments received from others. While people generally do become more anxious at the prospect of being videoed, they usually relax fairly quickly if it is used consistently. Audio-taping facilities are essential. Ideally, each role-play should be audio-taped and used in the ensuing discussion to provide examples of statements and responses. Each triad needs their own audio-taping and playback machine.

Timetabling. The workshop sessions can be run over a series of evenings, a series of half-day training sessions, over a couple of days, or over a weekend. The availability of time between sessions for homework practice allows consolidation of the learning of each skill to take place. Restrictions on time are generally imposed by the constraints of the financing body or the participants may only be available at certain times, as may the organisers themselves. If participants are having to travel from afar, then two consecutive days might well be the only sensible approach to carrying out the training. Whatever the duration of the programme, each participant needs to make a clear commitment to attend all sessions - this is part of their contract.

66

In planning this basic training programme, a minimum of five 'sessions' are required. Each of the first four sessions is related to a specific skill, while a fifth session is essential to combine the different skills into a coherent whole. Ideally, courses are run on five half day training sessions, each of about three to three-and-a-half hours duration. This allows ample time for people to warm-up and relax and to practise and discuss role-plays before moving on to the next workshop.

Materials. The essential materials required are the sheets presenting the description of the different basic skills, audio -taping facilities plus audio-tapes, a portable video system if possible, demonstration video-tapes if required and a flip-chart, blackboard or overhead projector. Spare paper and pens can be useful for those who wish to make notes (the observers will need to to this). Ivey (1983) has developed feedback sheets for use by observers which may also be useful.

These groups, as they develop over time, will tend to reflect normal group processes (see Rogers, 1970; Yalom 1975; Yalom 1983). Whilst it is inappropriate for a participant to use the workshop for 'free therapy', the fact that these sessions are concerned with experiential learning means that all the organisers will need to be acting in a facilitating role. Participants learn by taking risks and by exposing their strengths and the organisers must be sensitive to this. If any participant should move into personally distressing material it can be helpful if one of the organising team is available after the session to help that person cope.

Although the workshop focus is on counselling/ communication skills at the 'basic' level there will be many occasions throughout the sessions where the organisers act as models of live counsellors in the course of being available as facilitators. Aspects of this 'modelling' can usefully be acknowledged at appropriate times and provide teaching material of the more advanced skills of counselling. It is important for the organisers at the end of each session to discuss progress made and any issues arising, including those of group process.

WORKSHOP SESSION 1 : ATTENTIVE LISTENING: COMMUNICATING ATTENTION AND PROVISION OF MINIMAL ENCOURAGEMENTS TO TALK

When the participants arrive they are likely to be feeling tense, uncertain about what the immediate future holds in store for them and whether they are going to like it. Unbeknown to them this could well be what the members of the team are feeling too, but it is their role to help the newcomers feel welcomed and relax a little.

Introductory Activities
After a period of warm-up, group members join in the first

formal exercise. It is designed to help them get to know each other and recognise the relevance of listening skills. People are asked to work in pairs, choosing as a partner someone whom they do not know (or, if many of the group are already acquainted, someone whom they do not know well on a personal level). Their task is to introduce themselves to their partner by speaking about themselves for five minutes. The partner's task in this period is simply to communicate their interest and to listen and to speak only to clarify something they have not fully understood. After five minutes, the pair change roles, with the previous 'listeners' now introducing themselves to their partners. Organisers should also make themselves available for this exercise. At the end of ten minutes the pairs are asked to come together in the plenary group and sit in a circle so that all can see each other easily. Each person in turn is then asked to introduce to the whole group the person to whom they listened and to summarise briefly what they have learned of them. The task of the person being introduced is to listen to what is said about them and give feedback on its accuracy. In addition, they should comment on the inferences made by the talker on what was actually said. It is respectful to suggest people check out with their partners before reporting back whether anything has been mentioned which they would prefer not to share with the whole group.

The organisers need to be attending carefully to each participant in this plenary session (as in others). Cues will be observable about levels of discomfort, interaction styles and possible areas of unease which might well be overcome without help as the person relaxes, or might usefully be raised at a later point. Acceptance and acknowledgement of the reporters' attempt can be offered by the organiser.

It is often useful to play a naming game. This may also help to diffuse tension. In the circle, person A introduces himself-herself, then person B (next to person A) introduces himself/herself and person A. So it continues with, for example, person F introducing themselves, then running back through the introduction of E, D, C, B and A. Once the end of this line is reached, the game is continued with each person introducing everybody and getting faster each time until all are exhausted!

It is useful to clear the air of present but unvoiced concerns and expectations. Going around the group, organisers included, each person is invited to state their own expectations of and anxieties about the course. If there is someone who has been volunteered against their wish, they may find it difficult to relax and join in freely. This can place limitations on what they are likely to gain from the workshop and on what they can offer to others. The person could be asked if they are willing to let themselves try the first session constructively and if it is not to their liking to consider the option of dropping out of the group. At a suitable later

opportunity this issue needs to be taken up with their particular organisation.

An exercise that can be used, time permitting, is to ask
each group member to spend a few minutes considering what the
term 'counselling' (or 'therapy', 'interviewing', or 'communication', depending on the client group) means to them. Each
person could be asked to write down their definition and then
share this with the group - the organiser should highlight
similarities and differences between these definitions.

Reading Material
The material provided to each participant includes the
following:

Through carefully attending, the interviewer not only gains
valuable information but also conveys respect to the client,
communicates interest in what is being said and so encourages
that person to talk more openly and move to talk about areas
of more central concern. If the interviewer talks too much he
or she will have difficulty learning about the client. Carefully attending to the client means focusing not only on the
cues coming from the client, but also on the cues which the
interviewer gives out.

There are five main areas interviewers need to be aware
of in achieving effective attending behaviour:

Body language. If the interviewer is slouching in a chair,
looks bored and stares blankly out of the window they are not
likely to encourage the client to keep talking to them about
personally intimate matters. Both client and interviewer convey much through their posture and if the interviewer looks
attentive, clients are far more likely to speak about areas of
personal interest (and thereby maintain the interviewer's
attention). Many counsellors would say that clients know their
interviewers are interested if they sit leaning slightly forward, half-facing them, holding an interested expression on
their face and use encouraging gestures where appropriate. Such
a position is awkward to hold over a long period when many
clients are being seen. While such a position can be usefully
borne in mind, it is important that the interviewer feels
genuinely as relaxed as is relevant - that the client feels
comfortable and has a natural posture. This enables the
interviewer to concentrate more freely on the client.

Observation of clients' body language reveals a considerable degree of important information. An open, relaxed posture
suggests that is how they are feeling at that moment in time.
Apparent uncomfortable shifting in the chair, combined with
speech hesitations, stammering, breathing changes, etc., can
suggest a potentially distressing issue is being dealt with.
Facial behaviour also reveals much non-verbal information and
particularly important to notice is discrepant non-verbal

69

behaviour. An example of this is a person who, through tightly clenched teeth, growls menacingly 'I am not angry'.

Eye contact. Basically, if an interviewer wishes to express interest in someone, then he or she needs to look at them, initiate and maintain fluctuating degrees of eye contact with them. Clients will look at their interviewer from time to time to check out how they are being received. They need to see gentle, attentive interest, but not such an intensity of gaze that they look away out of discomfort. Interviewers can also usefully become aware of messages conveyed by client's eye contact. Does the client look away when particular issues are discussed? Similarly, interviewers also convey this information to clients through their own eye contact.

Vocal qualities. A considerable amount of information is conveyed not through what is said, but how it is said. The rate of speech, pitch, loudness and timbre of the person's voice speaks volumes. Try saying 'I love you' in as many different ways as possible and it is easy to recognise that often it is not so much what is said that matters, but how it is said.

The interviewer will convey much through his/her tone of voice, in addition to learning much from attending carefully to the client's vocal qualities.

Verbal tracking. This is a most powerful skill. It is closely allied to the skills of paraphrasing, summarising and questioning to be dealt with later. Verbal tracking is all to do with staying with the client's topic and verbal content, not introducing new variables or the interviewer's own inferences about what the client is meaning, leading to, etc. Interviewers, by confining their comments and questions to the topics and content of the clients' speech not only encourage the clients to talk further about the issue but also reinforce their dawning sense of self direction which leads to more spontaneity and frequently a greater sense of self worth. Where the interviewer adopts the role of 'the responsible expert' (which has its valid place in some settings), external boundaries of what is acceptable to discuss are immediately placed on the client. The clients also rapidly learn that the interview will be directed for them and that, therefore, in effect the interviewer is assuming responsibility for resolution of the issues under examination. Left to speak for themselves, clients will direct the topic to the central issues of concern when they feel secure in the interview.

Attending interviewers will quickly realise that the client gives much information, so much so that when it is relevant to give a response the interviewer is often spoiled for choice. Which bit should·be selected for further attention? Generally, the client will choose, but if ever the interviewer is stuck all he/she need do is first relax, then make a brief

comment on what the client has just, or very recently said.
There is no need to attempt to direct the client by introducing
a new topic. Verbal tracking is a powerful skill to use.

To summarise, the interviewers' aim is to maximise the
clients' time of talking (and cut down their own) by communicating their attentiveness primarily through use of body posture, eye contact, vocal qualities and tracking of verbal content.

Provision of minimal encouragements to talk. In line with this
aim is the interviewer's use of minimal encouragements to talk.
These convey to the client that he/she is attempting to understand and appreciate what the client is saying and also to
continue their expression. In effect they communicate 'I'm
with you, go on'.

Once the client has begun to talk in the interview, the
interviewer need only say a minimal amount to facilitate
continuation of expression. This word 'minimal' refers to both
the amount said, or expressed non-verbally, through gestures
by the interviewer and the degree of direction imposed by the
interviewer on the client. For example, consider interviews
you have had and think of the degree of direction imposed on
them. Did it inhibit you? Many interviewers do not realise the
powerful use of these minimal encouragements and continue to
unknowingly strongly influence the direction, content and value
of the interview.

These minimal encouragements take the form of simple
'Mmmm's' or 'Uh-huh's', repetitions of one or two key words
from what the client has just said (note the importance here
of accurate verbal tracking and appreciation of vocal
qualities), one word or simple questions ('Oh?', 'So?', 'And then?')
designed to allow the client to open up this topic further
('How do you feel about that?' 'What does that mean to you?'
'Tell me more, give me an example').

Demonstration Of The Skill

After discussion of this material comes the observation of a
demonstration of 'good' and 'bad' models of these particular
skills. It is not, of course, possible to present only these
skills in isolation and so the group must be encouraged to
focus particularly on the impact of the specific skills about
which they have just been reading. There then follows the demonstration of the skill on video or in-vivo, as mentioned
earlier, whichever method is being used.

Role-Play
The group now separate into sub-groups consisting of three
persons. The organiser describes the three roles (interviewer,
client and observer) to be assumed. The interviewer's role is
to speak minimally and to attend to their own and the client's
behaviour. The role of 'client' is something of a misnomer at

this stage. The aim of the triad is to help the 'interviewer' reach a degree of competence in these skills by their behaviour which should be supportive of the interviewer's attempts. This can be done by the 'client' talking, for example, about an area of personal interest. The observer's role is to observe the interviewer's attempt and the impact of his/her actions on the client. The organiser oversees the whole process.

The main difficulty encountered by 'interviewers' at this stage is relinquishing the sense of responsibility held for the client. It is often difficult to relax and 'just' listen, there is a temptation to ask question after question. Interviewers who ask repeated questions could be gently reminded by the organiser to relax and concentrate on attending to the client.

At the end of each role-play, feedback is given. All three participants share their thoughts and feelings. Feedback should focus on people's strengths and should be helpfully constructive, not negatively destructive. It should also be non-judgemental and focus on behavioural specifics. For example, 'You maintained eye contact much of the time, including one period where your client appeared particularly uncomfortable' is more easily received by an interviewer than 'You stared her into a state of fright!'. If video or audio-recording is used this can be an excellent prompt for feedback discussions.

Roles are then changed within the triad and the process continues until each member has assumed each role. Organisers need to be alert to participants' strengths and weaknesses in order to gently facilitate exploration and development during feedback sessions and later discussions.

After a short break for refreshment and relaxation with the same personnel, the process is repeated. It can be useful prior to the role-play beginning, for the interviewers to remind themselves (and be reminded), of the issues just discussed, on which they need to focus for their own development.

Ending The Session
A plenary group discussion in which feedback, comments and ideas are explored brings the session to a close. Participants are asked to undertake 'homework' to be reported on at the beginning of the next session. The homework task is to take each element of the skills comprising attentive listening and see how its manipulation affects personal encounters outside the group. For example, in a conversation with someone eye contact could be stopped for a while, attempts can be made to hold unflinching eye contact, or the effects of variable eye contact monitored and the effects of doing each of these noted.

WORKSHOP SESSION 2 : THE USE OF 'OPEN' AND 'CLOSED' QUESTIONS

Before the training activities begin, participants are asked for feedback on the previous sessions and on their homework.

## Reading Material

The material provided for session two includes the following:

In counselling orientated interviews the client generally arrives with something in mind to talk about. Given an accepting atmosphere and some time and space, clients will often be able to unburden themselves. This is not the time for the interviewer to stage an unwitting takeover bid for responsibility for the nature and content of the session and the direction it is going to take. By bombarding the client with questions this is exactly what the interviewer does. By gentle use of appropriate open questions and use of the other basic listening skills, interviewers can facilitate clients in relating their generally painful and often untold stories.

An open question is one which points the client towards an area of focus, but does it in such a way as hardly to limit the client's freedom of choice of reply. It enables and encourages the client to be self-directing in selection of the important, personally relevant issues to be discussed. It is only too true that the client is the only real expert on his/her self in these matters, any attempt to take over that role by an outsider undermines the client. Asking an open question generally leads to information, rich in quality, on how the client perceives his or her own personal situation. This encourages further exploration and in turn provides a more accurate understanding for the interviewer of the client's inner appreciation of the world, the client's internal frame of reference. Open questions invite clients to talk freely and are asked in order to help clients understand themselves more.

Closed questions, on the other hand, severely restrict the range of possible answers the client has to choose from. In the extreme they leave a client the option of only a Yes/No answer. Whilst the use of closed questioning can be argued as valid in establishing factual data, their unwitting or over usage can seriously hamper the interviewer's attempts to establish a safe and accepting atmosphere in the session which is essential for clients to feel able to engage in personal exploration. Too often closed questions are asked really to provide information to satisfy the interviewer's curiosity, not to help the client. Furthermore, biased closed questioning frequently will provide the 'right' answers to support the interviewer's personal theoretical orientation, enabling classification and depersonalisation of the client to take place. Use of questions becomes seductive too. While thinking of the 'right' question to ask next; and while trying to find 'The Ultimate Question' - which will provide that elusive bit of the psychological jigsaw and allow the 'Expert' to dispense correct advice - it is all too easy to either forget or be unable to concentrate adequately on the client's response to the question the interviewer has just asked.

So open invitations to talk are extremely useful in a

number of situations. At the beginning of the interview they
allow the client to state what is important to spend time on -
'What would you like to talk about today?' or 'How are things
going for you?', or 'How have things been since we last met?',
etc. Open questions facilitate client exploration of the issue
under consideration - 'How did you feel about that?', 'What
does that mean for you?'. They are most effective in eliciting
examples of specific events so that the interviewer is better
able to clearly understand what the client is describing - 'Could
you give me a specific example?' (this is probably the most
important question), or 'How do you mean having a bad turn?',
'What do you mean when you say there's a way out for you?', etc.
Effective open questioning builds upon the earlier attending
skills, and is much based on the interviewer's accurate tracking
of the client's verbal content and non-verbal messages.

Closed questions do have their use for gathering factual
information where necessary - 'What sort of pills did you take?',
or 'How long have you felt unable to catch a bus?', 'Can you
go into the front garden without feeling anxious?'. But beware
of the reasons for using closed questions. Is their use for the
interviewer's or client's benefit?

## Role-Play
After these paragraphs have been read and discussed, the role-
play for this skill begins. Participants are asked to form
triads once more, but are encouraged to select new partners so
as to facilitate variety in feedback. The role-plays progress
as in the first session. There is sometimes a tendency amongst
newcomers to this style of interviewing to ask many closed
questions and participants often find this session difficult.
Participants need to be encouraged to support and help each
other and to provide honest constructive feedback to the
interviewers. Organisers need to be alert to increasing frustration levels and reluctance by participants to relinquish well
established patterns of behaviour. The organisers can usefully
facilitate expression of the more negative feelings if they
occur. Sometimes some group members may blame their frustration
on the skill under consideration, or the teaching technique
used. This can reduce participants' motivation to perform the
task in hand and the organisers must decide if it is relevant
to suggest calling a halt to the exercise and beginning a frank
discussion of the difficulties arising. Occasionally, dissatis-
faction can be projected on to a particular member of the group
and this person becomes scapegoated.

In the closing discussion participants are encouraged to
examine their thoughts and feelings regarding the session. Many
of these might well have been explored in earlier discussion.
Time needs to be available for this work. If one triad has
dealt with some of these matters, but the others have not, it
is useful for one of the members of the triad to be asked to
report back to the rest of the group what happened. This

generally brings to the surface other people's similar experiences. Once more, homework is set. This time it is to practice
observing the effects of different questioning strategies outside the sessions.

WORKSHOP SESSION 3 : PARAPHRASING AND SUMMARISING

The same structure is adopted as for each of the previous
sessions. Observation on the previous sessions and on the
homework are invited. It is important throughout the workshop
that each participant feels his or her contribution is regarded
as valid and adequately heard. In effect the organisers act as
counselling role-models for the participants in this respect.
Participants are much more likely to be receptive to constructive criticism and open to attempting change of behaviour from
such a position of confidence. Whilst it is important to recognise and deal with group process issues which might be
brought up for discussion early on in the session, it remains
necessary to work on the skill which is the focus for the
session. The organisers may need to call a temporary halt to
discussion of process issues to enable exploration and practice
of the next building-brick in counselling skills acquisition.

Reading Material

The material provided in this session includes the following:

Attentive listening - careful attending behaviour and provision
of minimal encouragements to talk - communicates the interviewer's interest in the client and so encourages further
exploration. The skills of active listening - careful use of
questioning strategies, paraphrasing and summarising, reflection of feeling (to be examined in more detail in the next
session) - communicate to the client that he/she is being
understood and allows the clients to hear their own messages
more clearly.
    Both paraphrasing and summarising rely heavily for their
effectiveness on the interviewer's accurate verbal tracking
ability. They differ basically in the time span of the content
covered.
    Paraphrasing is the repetition to the client of the
essence of what has just been said. It is not repeating in
parrot fashion the client's own utterances, as can sometimes
form useful minimal encouragements. Some of the client's own
words can, of course, effectively be used in a paraphrasing
response though largely the interviewer uses his/her own words.
However, it is both an opportunity for the interviewer to check
out that the client's message is being accurately perceived
and an opportunity for the client, recognising the interviewer
is receiving the message accurately if this is indeed the case,
to hear their own message more clearly. This leads on to

further exploration and often to development of a fresh,
insightful appreciation of the issue.

Paraphrasing responses can be effectively made relatively
frequently in the interview, though not as often as minimal
encouragements. They are often delivered in a slightly questioning manner. They are most certainly not vehicles for introduction of the interviewer's own views on the topic. They are
opportunities to present the verbal content message to the
client. Some examples of paraphrasing are:

Client — Everyday there's something new to choose
from. There's football, tennis, swimming,
even judo and fencing.

Interviewer - There are plenty of activities to choose
from.

or

Client So if I take the job I threaten our relationship. But if I don't I'm going to stay
so depressed and then we just fight.

Interviewer - Whichever way you turn you seem to lose, is
that right?

When accurate paraphrasing is presented the client will often
respond with a version of 'Yes, that's right...' and move on
to explore the area further.

When an interviewer summarises, the time span of clients'
delivery of the material involved is generally greater, as is
its quantity. Large chunks of information can be summarised,
even whole interviews. Whereas paraphrasing statements tend
to be fairly short sentences, summaries can be much longer.
Again, the aim is to restate the client's own message, not the
interviewer's theoretical interpretation of the client's situation. Again, its use is varied, as a perception check for the
interviewer, as feedback to the client on the interviewer's
accuracy and the client's own messages. Often the summary
presents the client with views already expressed but in a more
coherent and integrated manner. An underlying theme might have
been returned to at various points in an interview (or even
over several interviews) and the summary can sometimes pull
facets of the client's perception of the issue together in a
manner not previously recognised. Because comparatively large
chunks of information are being dealt with, it is important to
conclude the summary with an enquiry regarding its accuracy
(such as '......is that it?', or'......does that sum it up?',
etc.).

Demonstration Of The Skill
Once more, after relevant questions, the group observes the
video or role-play demonstrations of both how effectively to
paraphrase/summarise and how ineffectively to do it, before
separating into triads.

Role-Play
By this stage it is likely that some participants will be
seeking suggestions for topics for the client to discuss. While
it is useful if an element of personal involvement in the role
exists - as it makes the role-play considerably more realistic
when genuine emotions and views are involved - it can be unfair
to both interviewer and client to use the opportunity for
expression of deeply personally distressing material. The
workshop organisers can usefully be armed with several slips of
paper, each outlining a particular circumstance in which the
client finds themselves and giving hints on how to develop the
role. Such scenarios can be geared to the type of situation
likely to be encountered by the participants and should
represent both more positive as well as problematic situations.
Being the third session and half-way through the workshop, now
is a useful time to invite participants to review their
strengths and weaknesses, in addition to dealing with other
issues of importance to participants.

WORKSHOP SESSION 4 : REFLECTION OF FEELINGS

Reading Material
This includes the following:

Effective practice of this skill builds upon all those preced-
ing it in the course of the workshop, particularly those of
accurately tracking the vocal qualities and non-verbal cues of
the client. Within western society there is considerable
emphasis on the intellect and a relative denial of the
importance of a person's feelings. The interviewer's noting and
appropriate reflection of these can often act as a re-
introduction for the client to a part of him/herself whose
importance has long been neglected.
    In the end the interviewer aims to communicate to the
client, 'I am accurately understanding and appreciating the
world as you perceive it, I'm in tune with how you think and
feel about things. Carry on further'. Reflection of feeling,
combined to an extent with reflection of meaning, completes
this aim. There is an art in accurately perceiving the client's
feelings and in conveying them to the client. In some areas the
client will be fully in touch with his/her own feelings and the
interviewer's reflection style needs to be aware of this (or
risk responses such as, 'I know I'm angry, what the hell are
you saying that for?'. At least such an angry response both
confirms the accuracy of the interviewer's reflection and
facilitates the client's expression of the emotion). Often,
though, the client is dealing with issues where the accompany-
ing feelings are ambivalent and therefore considerably more
confused to both the client and the interviewer. At such times
reflection needs to be gentle and almost questioning in its
manner. For example, 'It leaves you feeling beaten but angry,

is that right?'.

The key to effective picking up of emotional cues is to distinguish between verbal tracking, tracking of vocal quality and non-verbal behaviours. A person's body-posture, level of eye contact and particularly their vocal qualities change with their emotional experience. Tracking the verbal content fastidiously leaves little opportunity to focus on the emotional cues flowing from the client. Relinquish focus on the verbal content and tune into the emotional tenor of the encounter. As with any skill and certainly with all those which are the focus of these workshop sessions, the ability to use the skill develops in proportion to the amount of practice. In time it will be possible effectively to have one 'ear' on emotional tone, while the other continues to monitor the gist of the verbal content. Try relinquishing eye contact for certain short periods and focusing on the emotional tenor. Preface reflections to the client with the words 'You feel....'. It helps. Advanced reflection of feeling will sometimes, though of course not always, present a verbal content paraphrase in the appropriate emotional tone.

There is no need to constantly overdo reflection of feeling. Sometimes all that is necessary is a short reflection. As always, pace your responses to the client. Timing and degree of response are particularly important with this skill.

## Role-Play

The usual format is adopted, with demonstration of the skill followed by role-play practice and a discussion period. Organisers need to be particularly aware of the participants' own emotional tone in this session as some participants may feel personally challenged. In this session those participants who role-play invented and non-personally revealing scenarios will place their interviewees at a disadvantage. It can be worth reminding participants that the subject-matter for role-plays need not necessarily be an upsetting, miserable occurrence, but can be exhilarating and happy too. The homework task is given: to be more aware of the impact of reflecting feelings.

## WORKSHOP SESSION 5 : SKILLS INTEGRATION

Although a similar format is adopted in this session, there is no reading material per se. Instead the time available is spent in longer role-plays and extended discussion period. Extended role-plays are particularly relevant as from now on the practice of these skills will demand smoothness of integration of the component parts, exactly like in driving a car smoothly - the component skills are not in full conscious awareness but become more second nature as they are so well practised. The integrated real-life practice of these counselling skills relies not on the application of a set of techniques, but on a way of approaching an encounter with a client which is itself so well practised it becomes a genuine extension of that person's self. At that stage, the interviewer is more than ready to move on to learning more of the medium and advanced skills referred to earlier in this chapter.

There will be many issues which can be addressed in this final session - issues such as: 'Where do we go from here?' 'I feel I've just begun'. 'What happens if we make a mistake?'. Plus, of course, issues to do with termination of the group, which will likely be more apparent for some than others. Further training sessions can be attended by those pursuing involvement in counselling-related activities. If courses are not available then support and study groups could be set up to examine relevant issues and books. Newcomers to this field are helped by the organisers' open recognition that mistakes are made at times by all. Normally these will turn out to have no devastating effects as the client recognises the interviewer as human and places faith in the general atmosphere of the relationship which they have created together - this can and does survive powerful knocks. Occasionally, however, with some clients mistakes can have serious consequences. At that time it can be important to seek an opportunity for both personal support and objective examination of the situation.

One further issue to be addressed in the final session of the workshop is that of confidentiality. Counsellors are highly privileged to share other people's most intimate thoughts and feelings. This reflects a degree of trust which should never be treated lightly or abused. For some clients being able to establish an effective therapeutic relationship might form the only viable way out of their difficulties and if they are let down by one counsellor they might not seek another opportunity. It is necessary that participants appreciate fully the importance of respecting the confidentiality of the counselling relationship.

The workshop organisers will be working hard this session and can particularly usefully provide information on further aspects of counselling philosophy and approach, giving live examples from these sessions of where they have self-disclosed to the group, been empathic, confronted, etc. Participants can be invited to share how these experiences were for them and can derive considerable and important self learning from such exploration.

REFERENCES

Goldfried, M.R. (1980) 'Towards the delineation of therapeutic change principles'. American Psychologist, 35, pp. 991-999

Hobbs, T. (1986) 'Encountering Carl Rogers' Changes: Journal of the Psychology and Psychotherapy Association 4, pp. 182-137

Ivey, A. (1971) Microcounselling: Innovations in Interview Training, Thomas, Springfield, Illinois

Ivey, A. (1983) Intentional Interviewing and Counselling,
    Brooks-Cole, Monterey, California
Ivey, A. and Authier, J. (eds) (1978) Microcounselling:
    Innovations in Interviewing, Counselling, Psychotherapy
    and Psychoeducation, Thomas, Springfield, Illinois
Ivey, A., Normington, C., Miller, C., Morrill, W., and Haase,R.
    (1968) 'Microcounselling and attending behaviour: An
    approach to pre-practicum counsellor training', Journal of
    Counselling Psychology, 15, Part II - separate monograph,
    pp. 1-12
Kasdorf,J. and Gustafsen, K. (1978) 'Research related to micro
    training', in Ivey, A. and Authier, J. op. cit.
Llewellyn, S.P. (1984) 'The experience of patients and
    therapists in Psychological Therapy  unpublished Ph.D.
    Thesis, University of Nottingham, Nottingham
Llewellyn, S.P. and Hulme, W.I. (1979) 'The patient's view of
    therapy  British Journal of Medical Psychology, 52, pp.
    29-35
Luborsky, L., Singer, B., and Luborsky, I. (1975) 'Comparative
    studies of psychotherapies', Archives of General Psychiatry
    32, pp. 995-1008
Nelson-Jones, R. (1975) 'Personal Communication'
Nelson-Jones, R. and Patterson, C.H. (1974) 'Some effects of
    counsellor training  British Journal of Guidance and
    Counselling, 2, pp. 191-200
Parloff, M.B. (1976) 'Shopping for the right therapy',
    Saturday Review, 21.2.76, pp. 14-16
Rogers, C.R. (1942) Counselling and Psychotherapy, Houghton
    Mifflin, Boston
Rogers, C.R. (1951) Client-centred therapy, Constable, London
Rogers, C.R. (1957) 'The necessary and sufficient conditions
    of therapeutic personality change', Journal of Counsulting
    Psychology, 21, pp. 95-103
Rogers, C.R. (1961) On Becoming a Person, Constable, London
Rogers, C.R. (1970) Carl Rogers on Encounter Groups, Penguin,
    Harmondsworth
Rogers, C.R. (1978) Carl Rogers on Personal Power : Inner
    Strength and Its Revolutionary Impact, Constable, London
Sloane, R., Staples, F., Cristol, A., Yorkston, N., and
    Whipple, K. (1975) Psychotherapy versus Behaviour Therapy,
    Harvard University Press, Cambridge, Massachusets
Smail, D.J. (1978) Psychotherapy: A Personal Approach, Dent,
    London
Smith, M.L., Glass, G.V. and Miller, T.I. (1980) The Benefits
    of Psychotherapy, John Hopkins University Press, Baltimore
Yalom, I. (1975) The Theory and Practice of Group Psychotherapy,
    Basic Books, New York
Yalom, I. (1983) Inpatient Group Psychotherapy, Basic Books,
    New York

Chapter Five

TRAINING STUDENT HEALTH VISITORS IN HELPING SKILLS

SYLVIA RHYS

INTRODUCTION

The dynamics of the process of planning, running and assessing
workshops is the topic of this chapter and the theme running
through it is the leader as learner. The belief underlying this
theme is that the leader of a workshop, who is by the nature of
that role facilitating the learning of others, must also be a
learner in order to be effective as a leader.
    The chapter looks through the eyes of a leader, the author,
at the way in which she responded to the request to run two-day
workshops on helping skills for student health visitors.
Although health visitors had been among the participants of
previous workshops, it was the first time that the author had
run workshops exclusively for student health visitors and had
run workshops as part of a formal academic course. It describes
how she planned the first workshop, the workshop in action and her
reflections on it, and there are some comments also on a second
workshop which she ran for another group of student health
visitors some six months later.
    The reality of a workshop is highly complex and it is not
possible to convey to a reader the fullness of the experience.
The best that can be done is to make selections and to make
them in a systematic way. When selections are made from
reality, however, then reality is simplified and in this sense
distorted. This is an unavoidable difficulty which has faced
all the authors in this book. But, at the same time, this is a
legitimate and efficient way for an author to highlight for the
benefit of a reader certain aspects of an event which are
considered to be of particular significance.
    The basis on which the selection in this chapter is made
is that of decision-making. It is possible to view a workshop
as an interactional process involving a series of decisions on
the part of all participants (Nelson-Jones 1982). This does
tend, however, to suggest that there are rather more neat
cause and effect patterns in the dynamics of social interaction
than actually exist. The model is linear and so also is the

language in which we couch this, or any other model, for that matter. Language demands subject and predicate and a whole host of other grammatical rules, which render it relatively static (Palazolli et al 1978).

Social interaction, however, is perhaps better described as circular. We each analyse reality in our own terms and what appears to us to happen, or how another person appears to us to feel, becomes for us a fact. But it would be unlikely to tally exactly with the reality of that other person. The realities of each of us are strengthened or modified in the course of interaction with one another, but the degree of interrelatedness of our realities during the course of interaction varies.

This particular chapter concentrates on the reality of the leader and on a particular aspect of that reality, that is, on the leader in the role of the learner. It is hoped that this selection from and examination of, some aspects of the complexities of the workshop process may be of interest to other people who are involved in the process of running workshops and who, like the author, are constantly seeking ways and means of becoming more effective leaders. There may perhaps be some ideas and suggestions here which others can take and interpret and use in the context of their own realities.

THEORETICAL BACKGROUND: ADULTS AS LEARNERS AND TEACHERS

Adult Learning As A Shared Experience
'Through dialogue, the teacher of the students and the students of the teacher cease to exist and a new term emerges: teacher-student with students-teachers' (Freire 1972,p.53). According to Freire, education can have a liberating power when teacher and students share together their investigations of and seek potentialities for, re-creating reality. This fosters the development of creative intelligence. This outlook is very different from what he terms the traditional 'banking' approach to education in which students are regarded as the passive recipients of information which is selected by the teacher. Freire had in mind the underprivileged and oppressed peoples of the world, for instance, those of his native Brazil. But this principle, that learning in groups can best be undertaken as a shared enterprise, is one which, it is being increasingly realised, can be practised to advantage with adult learning groups in many different situations. It underlies the way in which the author approached the workshops to be described in this chapter.

Learning is about changing and taking new directions. During their lives, the knowledge, understanding, awareness, beliefs, judgement and insight of most adults continue to develop and change. The changes result from experience, from what adults see, hear, think, feel and do as part of the process of living in society. Some adults, however, over and above this incidental learning,make a conscious effort to educate themselves i.e. they take steps which are 'deliberate, planned and organised, undertaken with the conscious intention of bringing about change in knowledge, attitudes or skills' (Open University 1984, E355 Block A). From the work of Tough (1976) and many subsequent studies, it would appear that this process of planned education is more common than was once realised. Many adults have their own learning projects, that is, they make decisions about what they want to learn and then take steps to implement their decisions. They may seek information and advice from other people and from materials, such as books and television programmes, but they retain control of and responsibility for their own learning.

Knowles (1970) has suggested that the motivation for this planned learning is normally grounded in the roles which adults play in life. They come up against problems and challenges about which they wish to do something in order to alter their lives in some way. Their motivation might stem from their roles, for example, as house owners, e.g. how do I go about these various DIY tasks?; as parents, e.g. I need to know more about child development; as members of leisure clubs, e.g. I want to learn to swim/shoot/take part in amateur dramatics; as employees in paid work, e.g. I want to become a health visitor/improve my managerial skills/learn how to use the computer; as voluntary workers, e.g. I want to learn more about welfare rights/about the handicapped in the community, and so on. There are many adults, it would seem, who want freedom to learn about those aspects of living which are of particular importance to them at different stages in their lives.

This type of approach to adult education, which regards adults as capable of being active agents in their own development has been promoted by the humanist school of psychologists, e.g. Rogers (1969), Maslow (1970), Mezirow (1981). They believe that there is an innate drive in people towards an increased understanding of themselves and of the society in which they find themselves and of the people who make up that society. People are able to question hitherto taken for granted knowledge and ways of thinking, feeling and acting, and seek to change those aspects they regard as unsatisfactory. They can, if they have the motivation and opportunity, re-create their reality both by internal development, so that they view it through different eyes, and by taking steps to modify influences external to themselves. It should perhaps be noted, however, that this is not a universally accepted approach. There are those, such as Skinner (1981), who argue that human beings are moulded by the society of which they are a part and are not active agents in their own development.

Adults may choose to educate themselves on their own, with one other person, or in a group. Such learning may take place outside a formal institution, or adults may join, for example, a voluntary body, an evening class funded by a local education authority, or a university, as in the case of the students who took part in the workshop to be described in this chapter.

If learning is taking place in groups of two or more people, there is normally a division of roles between the teacher-student and students-teachers. But, as Freire's titles imply, this does not mean that the teacher necessarily opts out of the learning process while performing that role. Teachers have acquired expertise which they share with others. Rarely can it be said that a teacher has mastered that expertise to perfection, nor that the teacher has found the best way of sharing it with others. There is always more to be learnt. Teacher and students can choose to be jointly responsible for a process in which all grow. It is to this process of sharing that attention is turned next.

Adult Education And The Process Of Learning

Learning can be a risky business. This is because it involves change and change involves unlearning the familiar as well as learning the unfamiliar. New knowledge, new values, new feelings, new ways of going about tasks may upset that attitude filing system which we each have inside us and which gives order and stability to our lives (More 1974). Internal readjustments are likely to require also readjustments to the external world. The end product of learning can be liberation, as Freire suggests, a greater realisation of the potential of the self, but the process of learning may be fraught with difficulties, such as loss of self-esteem, loss of sense of direction, loss of sense of belonging with those with whom we previously shared so much.

Learning involves conflict as the student grapples with and tries to assimilate new knowledge, new feelings and so on. More (1974) describes it as a process of intellectual and emotional interplay. This interplay may last only a few moments, for some learning is relatively easily assimilated and requires only a slight modification to the internal filing system. But, at the other extreme, if the learning involves a shift in central values, then the conflict may last days, weeks, months, or even years. It may be accompanied by a whole range of emotions, such as anxiety, anger and depression before it is finally assimilated, the process being very similar to the mourning process, which is also an adjustment to fundamental change, as described, for instance, by Parkes (1972).

The task of a teacher is to help students to learn. Imparting information, the traditional activity of the teacher, is only part of this task. Learning, as suggested above, involves far more than simply acquiring new knowledge. A teacher cannot make students change or do their learning for them. What the teacher can do is offer opportunities for learning and a helping hand, if it is needed, to assist them through any conflict which may arise. How students use the opportunities on offer is their responsibility.

Teaching approached in these terms may be regarded as a form of counselling. The teacher, like the counsellor, provides

84

a relationship which enables students to help themselves and to
help one another. Assistance is offered to students to mobilise
their own resources, in the recognition that the person with
the difficulty is the one with the resources needed to deal
with it (Hopson 1982). The nature of the relationship between
teacher and students is thus important, for unless there is
mutual respect and trust it is not safe for needs to be revealed and for help to be given and received. This is a point which
Rogers repeatedly emphasises, e.g. '......the facilitation of
significant learning rests upon certain attitudinal qualities
that exist in the personal relationship between the facilitator
and the learner' (Rogers 1984). Seen in this light, the
teaching-helping process has much in common with the process
found in friendship and other helping contacts. Carkhuff and
Berenson (1977) have described counselling as a 'way of life'
and teaching, like counselling, is a specialised form of helping.

The balance of power between the one who is helper and the
one who comes to be helped is asymmetrical. The teacher can
exert considerable influence over the degree of asymmetry. For
example, the lecturer who comes into a room, talks non-stop for
an hour, then leaves, or the leader of a workshop who plans the
programme in detail in advance and sticks to it throughout the
workshop, are maximising the asymmetry of the balance of power.
In these situations, the students are not given any room in
which to express themselves, and be themselves, and work together
as a group. The teacher or leader concentrates on content,
thereby defining both what is to be regarded as useful knowledge and also the language in which it is couched; the
students are kept at a distance and expected to accept that
knowledge as it stands; they are not helped to translate it
into their reality. This is not to completely dismiss these
particular methods as such, but if they are taken to extremes
and become ends in themselves, then there is no room for the
development of relationships between group members. If the
learning process is shared, the power differential is decreased,
and teacher and students can talk to one another openly and
discuss their understanding of, their reactions towards, and any
problems they may have with the topic under study.

The teacher is the more powerful partner in the learning
process and has the greater say in deciding to what extent
power is to be shared. The less control the leader exerts over
a learning group, the greater the freedom people have to be
themselves and the greater are the uncertainties of the
learning situation for the teacher. On the one hand, it is not
possible to know how students are going to use the learning
opportunities on offer. They may perhaps welcome some and
reject others. Freedom means opportunities for students to
disagree and argue and enter into conflict with one another and
with the leader, as well as to agree and co-operate with and
help one another in their capacities as teachers. On the other

hand, there is uncertainty for the teacher because there are
no rules to determine how to act; like the students, the
teacher too has to decide how to make use of the freedom which
has been given.

Proctor (1978) has remarked 'It is the way that a
counsellor is with a person that matters'. If teaching is a
specialised form of helping others to learn in which relationships are important, then it is the way a teacher is with a
group that matters. If learning is indeed a risky business,
then an atmosphere of mutual trust and respect in which it
feels safe to venture into the unknown is necessary. Techniques
alone are not enough.

Adult Education And The Process Of Teaching
When teachers are learners as well as teachers, and students
are teachers as well as learners, the role of teacher as expert
is diminished and the role of student as problem-solver and
decision-maker is accentuated. If there is freedom for inter-
communication within a group, then the teaching/learning
process takes on the character of a kind of conversation in
which students' thinking and ideas are continuously utilised
as a means of moving forward (Holmberg 1984). How then can a
teacher establish and maintain this sort of guided didactic
conversation? Many different factors are likely to influence
the way in which a teacher approaches this task and their
sources may lie in the environment, in the students and in
the teacher. As regards environmental influences, for example,
if the only accommodation available is a small room, it is
difficult to hold simultaneous small group discussions or use
exercises which require a lot of space. The time available is
another influence on decisions on how to teach. It is not
helpful, for instance, to encourage the pursuit of new lines
of exploration in a discussion at a time when it is anticipated
the porter will be coming round to lock up. On the academic
side, it may be necessary to adhere in some measure to a
syllabus to help students prepare for some form of formal
assessment.

The size of a group of students usually has a bearing on
decisions made by a teacher on how to teach as does whether
that teacher has met group members before and is likely to
again. Different adults bring with them to a teaching situation
different characteristics, and these are so varied that it is
unlikely that a teacher can ever help all members of a group
to the same extent because different students are likely to
respond in different ways to the same strategy. Sometimes
it is even possible that some students will feel that they
receive little or no help.

It may be, for example, that some adults whose previous
experience of group learning has been confined to authoritar-
ian situations find it difficult to learn how to use freedom;
as adults used to making their own way in the world they may

be reluctant to expose what they regard as weaknesses and seek help with the learning process; and/or they may be taken aback to find that they can make contributions by virtue of their own knowledge and experience, thoughts and skills, to the learning process of others. If students have freedom, they can choose to use it actively, or to be passive.

Also, different adults have different learning styles. For example, it has been suggested that adults conceive of learning in different ways; some adults prefer surface level learning in which they focus on individual tasks for their own sake and adopt a relatively passive approach to their learning, while others prefer deep level learning in which they are actively concerned with understanding not only a particular task but also the meaning behind it and conclusions which might be drawn from it (Marton and Saljo 1984). Another way of conceptualising differences in adult approaches to learning is in terms of the stages being characterised by qualitative changes in thinking. Perry (1970), for instance, distinguishes nine stages; the adult at stage one adopts a passive accepting role to learning, believing all questions have simple answers which are right or wrong, while an adult at stage nine has recognised the relativity of knowledge and is willing to commit the self to a personal interpretation, expressing it through lifestyle. Differences such as those mentioned above may manifest themselves, for instance, in the type of contributions students make to discussions and the type of help which they seek from the group.

There are differences between students also at the tactical level. Some people, for example, prefer thinking visually, others like the opportunities for active experiences often used in workshops, while others may feel that they gain more from discussions. And in addition the degree of skill in learning itself varies considerably from one person to another. As Svensson (1984) has pointed out, skill in learning is not specific to the content of a particular course, but embraces the skills of understanding and of learning to learn.

Personal characteristics of a teacher influence the approach of that person to work. For example, different teachers have different assumptions and values on which they base their approach to their task, and the range of strategies and tactics on which one teacher draws varies from that of another teacher. How interested a teacher is in the content of the subject matter of a session and knowledge possessed about group processes are also likely to influence the approach made to teaching.

There can be no one best way to teach when so many different influences may enter into any one teaching situation. For the committed teacher this open-ended nature of the teaching process can be a challenge in itself. Reflection time after teaching can be particularly valuable as an opportunity for gathering together and weighing up thoughts and feelings.

Examples of questions which might be asked are: What has been learnt about how the students evaluated the session? Did they as a group find some aspects particularly helpful/unhelpful? With which aspects of the teaching process did the teacher experience confidence/difficulty? The next stage is thinking around the questions and answers, analysing which influences are of most importance and asking whether any action can be, or needs to be, taken. Some constraints, such as timetables, may not be capable of modification. But it may be possible, for instance, for a teacher to find a room of a different size, seek out different strategies and tactics to use at a certain stage, or stages, in the programme, or perhaps there are indications that there is a need to rethink certain assumptions underlying the teaching approach.

The teacher who engages in reflection before, during and after a particular task might be described in the words of Schon (1983) as a 'reflective practitioner'. Reflection in itself is an important skill which has to be learnt, and requires an ability to be aware of and weigh up not only people and circumstances external to the self, but also personal thoughts and feelings, and then to be able to integrate and apply constructively in practice what has been learnt. The skilled teacher must also be a learner and learning for teachers as well as for students can be a risky business.

PLANNING THE FIRST WORKSHOP ON HELPING SKILLS FOR STUDENT HEALTH VISITORS

Finding Out About The Students
Preparation began about two months or so before the date of the workshop. The leader had to make decisions on both the content and form it would take. Because it was being run for a specific group of students she thought it necessary to increase her knowledge of their course and of the work of health visitors for which they were being trained, and to speak to other leaders who had run comparable workshops.

All the students were state registered nurses, and had done midwifery or obstetric training. At the time of the workshop, the author was conducting a research project into staff stress in a hospital unit and so had been talking to nurses and hearing from them about their training and their work in a hospital setting, as well as reading relevant literature. She had discussions with the tutor in charge of the Diploma in Health Visiting, looked at the syllabus for the Diploma and found out more information from another researcher and from the literature.

Health visitors work in the community and have regard for the medical, psychological and social needs of individuals and families. They have a wide range of duties and activities. For example, they give advice to expectant mothers; they visit all babies soon after birth and seek to ensure that their care is

adequate and the child is progressing normally, and they give
help and support to mothers; in the school health service they
are sometimes the principal link between the school, the
family doctor and other agencies and they may work as school
nurses and health educators; they identify old people who require support and help and give advice to them on health and
maintain contact with the family doctor; they visit and help
the chronic sick and handicapped and their families; they
undertake health education in the community, for example, in
old people's clubs, and they carry out screening procedures,
such as hearing tests for babies (Working Party 1969).

The leader was able to meet the first group of student
health visitors at only one workshop, so it was arranged that
she should have an hour's meeting with them about three weeks
before it took place. At the meeting, the leader explained that
in order to help her plan the workshop programme she would be
grateful if the group would be willing to tell her something
about themselves and the work they had been doing so far in the
course. After the leader and students had introduced themselves
to each other, a short small group exercise on the students'
understanding of the term 'counselling' served as a catalyst
for a group discussion on helping skills.

Content Of The Workshop
The workshop needed a theme to hold it together. 'Helping
skills' is a very wide assignment. There were no constraints
imposed by the tutor in charge of the course nor by the Diploma
syllabus, beyond the need for the content to be relevant to the
work of health visitors. As a result of her investigations
described above, the leader came to the conclusion that a useful theme would be that of communication, with particular reference to those skills which can be brought to bear on the
process of building up and maintaining a relationship with
another person or persons. Establishing such a relationship
with clients is likely to be an essential part, or the main
ingredient of the work of health visitors.

Communication is part and parcel of our everyday lives,
yet is too often just taken for granted. A number of writers
(e.g. Argyle 1981) have pointed out that the importance of
social skills is often underestimated. To be able to select the
skill most appropriate for any given helping situation, a health
visitor, like a teacher, has to be aware of and able to weigh
up influences whose roots may lie in the self, in other people
and in the environment. Students in a workshop have a chance to
study in a sheltered environment their own ways of communicating and those of others. They can use workshop exercises as
opportunities for reflection, self-assessment, experimenting
and discovery. This workshop was not part of the assessment
process associated with the Diploma course, except in so far as
the topic of helping skills is normally included in some form
in the written examination to be taken near the end of the

Diploma course. Because of this, neither the leader nor the students would be constrained by evaluation requirements and the leader would be able to promise that what was done and said would remain confidential, an important factor in establishing a climate of trust.

There were a number of other reasons why the theme of communication seemed appropriate to include in the Diploma course. All the student health visitors were trained nurses and, while communicating with others is an essential part of a nurse's job, her training rarely includes the study of the process as a subject in its own right (Bridge and Clark 1981). There is an increasing recognition of the importance of the psychological and emotional needs of patients as well as of their physical needs, and growing interest in applying the so-called 'nursing process' to planning patient care. A nurse's work, however, is mainly task initiated and relatively greater emphasis is placed on 'doing' skills. As one researcher has remarked, 'Nurses do things as their work....If they are not doing something physical they are not working' (Janes 1984). There is evidence to suggest that, while nurses might recognise psychological states, such as anxiety, the understanding is at a general level and they are not skilled in assessing the actual psychological needs of a particular individual (Watley and Muller 1984). It has been recommended that in all types of nurse training increased emphasis should be given to the development of elementary communication and human relationship skills (Counselling in Nursing 1978).

It would seem desirable for all nurses to have a range of tactics and strategies in communication at their disposal in order to be able to select those most appropriate in any particular situation and with any particular patient. It can be argued, however, that it is essential for health visitors to be versatile in communicating skills. They are engaged in preventive and developmental rather than curative work, and they are likely to have on their caseloads at any one time a much greater variety of clients with a wider range of problems than is a nurse on a hospital ward. Clients are likely to include different age groups from different classes and perhaps from different cultures. Health visitors often communicate not only with their clients but also with relatives and friends of clients whose ages and background and circumstances also differ widely. All these people themselves employ different styles of communication. Problems health visitors are likely to be presented with can vary from how to care for a newly born child to the psycho-social problems of the elderly. How a health visitor communicates is likely to have an important bearing on the quality of help offered. Even straightforward information can be presented in a variety of ways, some of which may encourage a client to make use of it and others to reject it.

In addition, a health visitor is likely to be the only health visitor with whom any particular client has a relationship, unlike the hospital patient who is cared for by a team of nurses. A health visitor may visit a home over a period of weeks, months, or even years, and different ways of communicating may be called for at different stages in this relationship.

Another important factor which calls for versatility in communication skills in the health visitor is the setting in which the communication takes place. Health visitors are not dealing with a captive audience on foreign territory, i.e. the patient in a hospital bed. They are often communicating with people on their own territory, i.e. in their home. They themselves are guests in those homes and yet at the same time they are professionals. The two roles may conflict. They cannot, in the way they might in a hospital, lay down rules and regulations for their hosts (McIntosh 1981).

It is also useful for health visitors to possess a range of communication skills which they can use to help each other as well as their clients. They often work in greater isolation than do hospital nurses. The work of home visiting, for example, they normally do on their own and time spent in communication with colleagues may be limited. All nurses are traditionally expected to be self-reliant and to cope unaided in whatever the circumstances (Counselling in Nursing 1978). This may well be connected with the fact that the majority of them are women whose traditional role in society is to be supportive of others. The giving of social support to others without receiving support oneself (the support gap), it has been suggested, is a source of stress to women today (Bell 1982). The problem of who cares for the carers is now being given attention in some quarters, e.g. by the establishment of CHAT, a counselling service for nurses, run by the Royal College of Nursing. On a day to day basis, however, it is important for health visitors to have opportunities for communicating with colleagues or other understanding persons.

Communication was to be the theme of the workshop. But many different skills come under this heading, for example, non-verbal skills, such as body posture; verbal skills, such as different types of questioning; cognitive skills, for instance, being able to follow the reasoning behind a client's words; affective skills, such as conveying to a client a feeling of warmth and respect. In two days it would be possible to work on only a very few of these. From her investigations generally, and in particular from what she learnt from the pre-workshop meeting, the leader concluded it was important to pay particular attention to non-verbal communication and to seeing individual skills in context as integral parts of the overall process of communicating in the field.

Structure Of The Workshop
The decisions which the leader took on the structure of the workshop were influenced not only by her thoughts on the

content of the workshop outlined above but also by the setting
in which the workshop was to take place, i.e. a large seminar
room with furniture which could be moved around, by her
theories and assumptions about adults as learner and teachers
which were outlined previously, by the information that she
learnt from another leader who had run a similar workshop, and
by her previous experience and her self-knowledge about her
capacity as a leader. She considered it important that the
learning process about communication skills should be shared.
Freedom would be necessary for the students to have opportunities for reflection, self-assessment etc., which has already
been referred to, and to think about how they might carry on
learning after the workshop was over. At the same time it was
necessary to strike a compromise between, on the one hand, the
need for covering ground relevant to the Diploma course and,
on the other hand, giving everyone as much freedom as possible
to pursue their personal needs.

The leader's overall strategy can be described as one of
'freedom within structure'. She decided that there would be a
number of exercises, each followed by opportunity for discussion. She decided also to prepare more than there would be time
for and to select from them those which seemed most appropriate
on the day. She would provide outline instructions for the
exercises, but how each developed would depend on the actions
and interactions of all participants. The students would be
free to make suggestions about modifying the exercises, or
adding new ones. While she had some ideas on the order in
which the exercises might be used, she was prepared to re-
arrange that order if it seemed advisable.

The leader also gave attention to the need to include
variety within the programme. This was partly because different
students have different styles of learning and she wanted to
cater for as wide a range as possible. In addition, different
tactics appeal to different people, some prefer thinking
visually, others like active exercises, while othes want
discussion. Some 'fun' exercises were included; they can be
useful not only to add variety but also to help break the ice
and to increase the level of arousal of participants so that
there is energy available to invest in gathering experience
and information (Van der Molen 1985). Variety in both type of
activity and in the pace at which activities were carried out
would also help to maintain the interest and concentration of
all concerned and to counteract any tendency to boredom. This
would be important not only for the students but also for the
leader.

The exercises which the leader prepared included some to
be carried out on an individual basis, some in pairs,
discussions in small groups and in one large group, writing,
compiling charts, listening to tapes and role-playing. She
arranged for two friends to come in to help with a role-
playing exercise during the second morning. This was the one

piece of timetabling to which the group would have to adhere. Some of the exercises the leader was familiar with, others she would be trying out for the first time.

This pattern of freedom within structure meant that the leader maintained a dominant role in defining in outline what was valid knowledge for her students (see Woolfe and Murgatroyd 1979 for a discussion on this topic) and in the general way in which that knowledge would be explored. But the details of the content and structure would be filled in by the group during the course of the workshop. As explained, no detailed programme was prepared in advance. The programme which is outlined in Appendix I took shape in the course of the workshop itself.

RUNNING THE FIRST WORKSHOP FOR STUDENT HEALTH VISITORS

Introduction
The workshop took place about half way through the students' twelve month diploma course and all the twelve students who took part had by then come to know each other quite well. Their ages ranged from the mid 20's to the mid 40's. Some came direct from hospital work to training for work in the community. Some had already had some experience in the community, e.g. as school nurses. Some came direct from full-time paid jobs, others with families were returning to nursing after a break of a number of years. Eleven of the students attended on the first day and were joined by the twelfth, who had been ill, on the second day. In addition, one trainee nurse tutor took part throughout the workshop. Two friends of the leader who took part in a role-playing exercise were present for part of the morning on the second day.

The workshop took place in a moderate sized room. The furniture could be moved around and there was room for a variety of activities, but pairs and sub-groups had to work in rather close proximity to one another. Coffee and tea breaks were taken in the room.

Appendix I summarises the programme which developed out of the interactions of the participants with each other and with the leader. It is possible, in retrospect, to discern six principal stages of development, which are described below. That the first stage would be climate setting and the last stage would be assessment and evaluation could be anticipated beforehand, but how many intermediate stages it might be possible to distinguish and the nature of them could not be known until the workshop had become reality.

What follows is a very brief summary, item by item, of a few aspects of the many happenings in the workshop over the two days. Making the selection was not easy. The aim has been to convey to the reader an outline picture of the main events in the workshop and to highlight a number of aspects which illustrate, from the leader's viewpoint, the processes both of facilitating learning in a workshop and also of learning from the workshop experience.

## Day 1
### Stage 1: Getting Down To Work
The workshop began rather tentatively. After two terms the
group members had come to know each other quite well, but had
not worked together previously in a workshop and were not sure
what to expect and they had met the leader only once before for
an hour.

The leader introduced the workshop by describing the sort
of structure and the theme it would have and she explained
briefly the teaching/learning principles which she had in mind.
This led on to a consideration of the type of contract which
would exist between members of the group during the two days;
everyone would be responsible for their own actions and able
to choose how much to contribute to and take away from the
workshop. The leader explained it was no part of her role to
act as assessor; she was there to guide and to explore with the
group the topic in hand and there would be plenty of opportunity for discussion and comment. If anyone wanted to talk to her
on an individual basis, they would be very welcome to do so at
the end of each day, or during the day if it were urgent, or
contact her after the workshop was over.

The students listened very carefully and seriously and
there was some brief discussion. They then joined, if a little
hesitantly, in two group exercises. The first was a fun game
which helped to lighten the climate by engendering some amuse-
ment. In the second exercise which served to introduce the
topic of non-verbal communication, each individual acted non-
verbally an emotion for the others to guess. Some joined in
whole-heartedly, others a bit hesitantly in a type of activity
which was evidently new to them.

In the next exercise on non-verbal communication, the
students worked in pairs through some short exercises, following a set of written instructions. This type of activity
appeared to give a boost to their self-confidence. They followed the instructions carefully and quickly and in the discussion
which followed were willing to contribute examples from their
own experiences and the conversation was lively and full of
anecdotes. The subject matter was extended by the group to the
use of touch in different situations, with different types of
people and with people from different cultures. During the chat
over coffee several students remarked that they had not had an
opportunity for 'such a good natter' for a long time!

Coffee making itself (and tea making in the afternoon) was
organised very efficiently by the group, and after a not very
long break, members spontaneously tidied up cups etc. and
indicated that they were ready to restart. It was almost as if
they wished to show how efficient they were when they were in
charge. In this, and in other ways, they showed that they had
devised methods for working together as a group. For example,

during the course of the workshop, some of them would tease one particularly talkative person whenever it was felt that that person had gone far enough for the time being.

After the coffee break, the group itself initiated a follow-up to item 4 with a discussion on the pros and cons of having to wear uniforms in the course of their official duties. Again, it gave an opportunity for sharing personal experiences. The group members appeared much more confident by now that they could cope with the workshop.

Stage 2: Increasing Challenge Of The Learning Process
After the topic of uniforms had been explored for a while, the leader detected a general feeling of readiness to move on, and, having checked this out with the group, introduced another exercise, this time one on listening and carried out in pairs. It proved something of a challenge to a number of the students who found it very difficult to refrain completely from making comments while their partners were describing one of their cases. In the discussion afterwards, some students appeared confident that the process of communication with clients presented few problems, but some of the others began to admit to some difficulties which were worrying them, especially when they were visiting clients in their own homes.

After lunch, the warm-up exercise was being enjoyed enthusiastically by the group when it was interrupted by a member of staff working on the floor below, who complained about students larking about and was afraid that the ceiling would fall in! He was somewhat taken aback to find the leader also 'larking about' and rather bewildered to hear that having fun was part of the learning process! It was an interesting illustration of how learning is normally regarded as a serious and primarily passive activity.

After making a few amused comments on the interruption, members indicated that they were ready to get down to the more serious business of the afternoon. Item 10 on questioning was another exercise which presented the group with something of a challenge, this time as regards both the content and the nature of the exercise. The leader invited ideas about different ways of asking a client questions and suggested that the students might like to give a brief role-play to illustrate their ideas. That there may be different ways of asking questions was an idea new to many members of the group, and there was considerable reluctance to role-play in front of other group members. The two people who did volunteer gave a useful illustration of a health visitor who peppered a client with questions, leaving the client with little space in which to explain difficulties in her own way.

It seemed important to pause and to think around this topic. The leader added some ideas about types of questions which had not yet been covered. She was interested to note that in the discussion which followed, only limited attention was paid by group members to the difficulties there may be in gathering relevant information from clients and to the need to have a range of resources to use as necessary. There was a tendency to keep moving away from uncertainties in the process of communication as part of the helping process and to concentrate instead on practical difficulties, such as how to cope with a queue of patients at a clinic when time is strictly limited. In other words, there was a tendency to concentrate on coping with difficulties arising in the environment, rather than on the strategies and tactics which the students themselves might develop to influence others.

Item 11 began with an individual exercise in which members filled in charts with words which they considered described how they experienced particular feelings with different degrees of intensity. Group cohesion was by now becoming somewhat less marked. It seemed to be safer not always to swim with the current. The ensuing discussion both within and between the two groups into which the class split was vigorous and highlighted the fact that the same word used to describe a particular feeling may sometimes have different shades of meaning for different people. It follows that it is important for health visitors to cross-check meanings, particularly of what seem to them to be crucial statements, when talking with clients. Some students seemed somewhat dismissive of the significance of this, while others looked very thoughtful.

Division of opinion was again evident during the last exercises on the first day. There was time to listen to two short tape extracts, giving examples of contrasting styles of conducting initial interviews (item 13). (The parts of the counsellor in the two extracts were taken by trainee counsellors and the clients were role-played). Some students thought the counsellor on one tape too passive and said they would have got up and walked out if they had been interviewed by someone who sat there and said virtually nothing. One or two were particularly indignant when the client exclaimed 'I feel awful about this. I ought to be able to cope', because the counsellor did not respond by comforting the client. They wanted to apply their way of helping with physical difficulties to helping with emotional difficulties. Another student pointed out how important it was to give the client a chance to express herself. The leader took the opportunity to encourage this line of thought and suggested there may be times when it is important to give opportunities to clients to formulate, reflect on and accept their own ideas and feelings.

Some of the strongest feelings were expressed by some students who said they recognised that they identified in some way with the client and/or the situations. This served, inter alia, as an opportunity to discuss how important it is for a helper to be aware that strong personal feelings may be triggered off in a situation and that if this happens it is necessary, in order to concentrate on the client, to recognise

those feelings, then to put them to one side for the time being
but not to try to ignore or repress them. The work for the day
ended with some pondering on this topic.

Day 2
Stage 3: Resuming The Task
Several of the group members began proceedings on the second
day by commenting on the interruption the previous day by one
of the staff and offered suggestions for an alternative venue
for future workshops. The leader thanked them for their
comments and suggestions and made a note of them. It was interesting that no one suggested that the activity itself was inappropriate, and indeed everyone willingly joined together in
another warm-up exercise, a less energetic one this time!

Empathy was one aspect of communication which the leader
had thought might be useful to work on during the workshop; it
had been mentioned several times during the previous day and
was of importance to the topic on which the day had ended, but
had not yet been the focus of attention. She now introduced a
short exercise (item 16) on empathic responding. Students
referred in the course of discussion to the work on non-verbal
communication and discussed for a time how what is said may
have different meanings according to how it is said. There
were some thoughtful comments on the importance of accepting
clients and not making them feel inferior, and on how this
might be achieved. There was not unfortunately, enough time
to give the topic of empathy as much attention as the leader
thought it merited as an essential, but not always easily
understood, aspect of the helping process. For logistic reasons,
it was necessary to fit in before lunch the role-play with
which two friends were helping.

Stage 4: Role-Play (Item 18)
The two visitors to the group role-played clients in two
different scenarios. In the first, they acted the part of
parents of a young child who was refusing to go to nursery
school. In the second, they were husband and wife finding
problems coping with an elderly relative who was living with
them. The two students who role-played the health visitors
experienced difficulties in coping with two pairs of very
uncooperative clients with multiple problems, deliberately
presented in this way to act as a challenge to the students.

The ensuing discussion plunged immediately into the prac-
ticalities of the two family situations. There were normative
comments on the behaviour and attitudes of these clients in
particular and of clients in general with similar presenting
problems and there was a plentiful supply of anecdotes and
personal experiences. Most of the interaction was between the
students themselves. They seemed to be looking to each other
for support when discussing two situations with which they
experienced difficulties.

The group needed the encouragement of one of the role-players and the leader to concentrate on process rather than on content. In the course of the discussion, the role-player challenged conventional polite methods of communication. He pointed out that presenting problems are not always the basic problems and suggested that the two couples in the role-play were playing games in which they looked for arbitrators rather than solutions and that perhaps their games should be challenged. There are times when it may be important to give clients permission to be angry and confrontation may be a constructive way of bringing conflicts into the open. Empathy is not about 'being nice', but rather it is about tuning into the world as it is.

As the group contemplated these ideas, some strong feelings began to surface. This way of communicating with clients seemed to run counter to the students' training as nurses and there were reactions of doubt and disbelief and some anger. One person asked incredulously 'Are you saying that you think we were being too polite?' It was again apparent that there was reluctance on the part of the students to recognise the power which they themselves could wield in their roles as helpers. There was a tendency, as in the exercise, item 10, to concentrate on how to cope with factors external to themselves, to the neglect of the influence which they themselves could exert on interactions with others. It was interesting, however, that by the end of the discussion a number of the students were beginning to look more closely at, and weigh up, what they saw as their own strengths and weaknesses as regards different ways of communicating.

Stages 5 and 6: Interlude And Assessment And Evaluation
After this hard work, the group enjoyed lunch together at a local hostelry to celebrate the end of term. This, together with the afternoon warm-up exercise, were welcomed as light relief.

Some of the variety and intensity of feelings which had appeared in the morning re-appeared when the students commenced the task of evaluating the workshop. They began by thinking about and evaluating their own helping skills and listing those which they already had, noting those which they thought they should improve and those which they thought they should acquire (item 21). In the course of the group discussion which followed, they highlighted some problems which they saw as associated with the process of helping. The main ones were coping with anger, coping with crisis, deciding whether they would be able to see a case through, and taking risks. There was some lively discussion on whether and when to confront; it appeared that in this respect the deeply held beliefs of some of the students about always trying to be 'nice' to people were being challenged. Of those skills they thought they needed to develop, attentive listening came at the top of the list for a number of them. This was followed by empathy, confronting coping with silences, guiding interactions, setting aside one's feelings, being aware of process as well as of content, and how to withdraw from and then evaluate situations.

This exercise was followed up after tea by an individual exercise in which the students wrote down the steps they intended to take as a result of attending the workshop. The steps they listed included practising analysing conversation, being more prepared to listen, not being afraid of silences, being more alert for non-verbal cues, improving communication tactics and strategies and weighing up more critically transactions between people.

In the final exercise the students again worked together as a group. They put forward ideas for future workshops for the next intake of students, which included suggestions on both content and structure. They seemed pleased to be able to round off the workshop by making these contributions, for which the leader expressed appreciation.

REFLECTIONS ON THE WORKSHOP

Introduction
This workshop was lively and energetic. It was difficult to convey in a short summary more than a hint of the complexities of the dynamics of the group in action over the two-day period. The workshop required a great deal of concentration on the part of the leader who was tired by the end of it. The great temptation then was to breathe a sigh of relief, and turn the mind to other things until it was time to prepare for the next workshop.

But an opportunity for learning is lost if relection on an episode does not take place while it is still fresh in the mind. The leader looked back over the events, at some jottings which she had made during the course of, and at the end of, each day and at the letters written by the students themselves at the end of the workshop. And she did the same after a second workshop which she ran six months later with another group of student health visitors. This was the first of two workshops, and the programme was rather different from that of the first workshop which was the only one in that particular academic year. While details of the second workshop are not provided here, it is useful to refer to events in it for comparison.

As it has been necessary to make selections from reality in order to describe the workshops in action, so it is also necessary to make selections from the process of reflection. The comments which follow on the next few pages are by no means exhaustive. There was so much to think about. How one evaluates a workshop is interlinked with what one is seeking to evaluate in that workshop. The selection here has been made by concentrating on the general theme of freedom within structure. This is not the only dimension along which the event could have been evaluated. The main purpose is to illustrate some aspects of the learning process in action after the event.

## The Workshop Process And The Students

The aim of the workshops was to provide opportunities for
student health visitors to learn more about helping skills.
Active learning may seem very strange to some people who have
been accustomed to sitting passively listening to the teacher,
or at most making a few contributions to a class discussion. To
be invited to join in a series of different exercises, to have
space in which to express opinions and thoughts and to be
encouraged to comment on the proceedings, can come as something
of a shock to the uninitiated, especially when the workshop is
an integral part of a course, the academic part of which is
taught on rather more conventional lines. It may take time to
become used to greater freedom to learn which is characteristic
of the workshop process.

Although there were some criticisms of individual items,
the leader found it interesting that there were no adverse
comments on this type of learning as a whole. The letters which
the students wrote at the end of the workshop concentrated on
gains they considered they had made as a result of attending
and how they would continue their learning; no one apparently
considered it a complete waste of time. They had entered into
the workshop proceedings as a whole with enthusiasm, differences had been expressed, information had been sought and there
was evidence that some attitudes had been challenged. As
regards possible future developments (item 24), the students
were emphatic that two two-day workshops would be useful during
the Diploma course, one during the first term and one during
the second term, then a study day about three weeks before the
final examination.

This did not hold true to quite the same extent, however,
for the second group of students after their first workshop.
They were allocated two two-day workshops. The first one took
place near the beginning of the first term. Words used to
describe it included 'interesting', 'stimulating', 'enjoyable'
and 'valuable', but it was evident that four of the sixteen
students had some reservations about the experience. Two of
them saw the games as a waste of time and wanted to observe
practical situations; one would have preferred more general
discussion, yet also said that a lot of time was wasted because everyone had different ideas; one would have preferred
more observation and thought workshop exercises underlined
present behaviour without bringing about modifications. Another
student, however, described a change of attitude towards this
type of learning during the workshop itself; initially she
felt slightly hostile, but by the end of the second day she
felt she had learned more about herself than any formal lesson
would have achieved. It seemed to the leader that there was a
need to give this second group of students an opportunity, if
they so wished, to spend time at the beginning of their second

workshop discussing workshop learning and voicing any doubts and misapprehensions they might have. She wondered whether in the following year she might perhaps encourage students to think more about the process of active learning during the actual course of their first workshop.

The leader thought it might be useful also when deciding which type of exercise to use at which stage in a workshop to pay rather more attention to the need to grade more gently the transition towards less structure and greater freedom. For example, in the exercise on non-verbal communication (item 4) at the beginning of the first workshop, she noted that the students had responded very readily to written instructions. She reflected that this could be looked at in two ways. On the one hand, it might be regarded as a tactic which could be used again with other groups of student health visitors as a means of getting a workshop going. On the other hand, perhaps it was insufficiently stimulating, following instructions correctly becoming an end in itself rather than a means to an end. She did not use this method in the second workshop, but after it was over she thought that it might well have been a useful type of exercise to use again, especially at the beginning of a workshop for students just starting on their course when they were feeling as yet somewhat insecure working as a group.

By way of contrast, spontaneous role-play is an activity in which there is greater freedom from formal rules than in many other activities. Students are asked to concentrate on the informal rules of everyday life, a risky venture possibly for some who might feel that their integrity as adults is at stake. It certainly appeared to present something of a challenge to the students in both workshops. In the first workshop only one pair of students took up the invitation to role-play (item 10). In the second workshop students were doing an exercise in groups of three on the afternoon of the first day, and this time only one group out of five decided not to role-play and two of the students in that group subsequently indicated some regret about this. Role-play is a valuable tool which can be used both to examine current ways of communicating and also to try out new ones. The leader thought that in future workshops, she would perhaps postpone role-play to the second day and might try offering a little more guidance in the form of very brief written outlines of roles, as was done in the workshop on bereavement (chapter 6) although keeping exercises much less elaborate than in that workshop.

The leader wondered whether perhaps some people, such as nurses, whose training emphasises the need to respond to stimuli in the environment rather than to internal stimuli, may need a little more encouragement to learn how to use freedom in learning. In the first workshop, one feature which the leader noticed was that the students' underlying outlook tended to be in terms of reacting to a set of circumstances. They were inclined to look for lists of symptoms or factors in the environment to which they could respond, for example, items 10 and 18. The students said, however, that they saw the move to the community as an opportunity to gain greater autonomy. In the second workshop the students did an exercise in which they looked at differences in the way in which they approached their work (or anticipated they would approach it) in a community as compared to a hospital setting. Again it became apparent that the desire for greater autonomy was an important reason for the move to the community.

It would seem that an important motivating factor for nurses behind their decisions to become health visitors is likely to be a desire for more freedom from structure within their professional work. Perhaps more attention should be given to this factor and to implications for professional/client relationships stemming from it of which students were not yet fully aware. The more freedom from structure a helper has, the greater the choice which can be exercised about how to act and how to use the power he/she possesses vis-à-vis the client, and it is important to continually pay attention to this aspect of inter-relationships. The leader wondered whether the theme of the relative importance of internal and external loci of control might be a useful one to incorporate into a future workshop.

The above reflections arise out of thoughts about the characteristics of the two learning groups as a whole. It has to be borne in mind, however, that no two groups are ever alike. Each is made up of people who bring to bear on the learning task his/her unique individual characteristics in the form of previous experience, knowledge, styles of learning, skills in learning and preferences for different strategies and tactics etc. The greater the freedom within the learning situation, the more apparent the differences are likely to become. It was noted in the first workshop how group cohesion gradually became less pronounced as time went on. A leader can look for recurring overall patterns to use as guidelines in future workshops, but there is a need for flexibility within these guidelines to cater as far as is possible for the individuality of groups and of the learners who comprise them.

The Workshop Process And The Leader
As well as reflecting on the students in relation to the concept of freedom within structure, the leader thought around her own role.

Had her decisions resulted in a satisfactory balance between freedom and structure? There could be no definitive answer to this question. On the whole the leader could find no very good reasons for thinking that it should be changed to any substantial extent, but it was an issue to be kept in mind for future workshops because it is so fundamental. The students had joined in the exercises willingly, spontaneous role-play being the only one in which there had been some reluctance.

They had developed the exercises with apparent interest, had been eager to enter into discussions afterwards, and had initiated one item, the discussion on uniforms, themselves. The initial hesitancy and uncertainty had gradually broken down and some students took up opportunities to debate issues of fundamental importance to their thinking, and some strong feelings had been displayed. The leader noted that in both the first and second workshops the fact that proceedings were confidential helped to establish a climate of safety; a few students checked out at intervals that particular remarks of theirs would not be passed on.

In the course of the workshop the leader had played a variety of roles, for example, speaker when she was introducing the workshop, then gamesplayer, socialiser, organiser of individual items and the programme as a whole, facilitator during discussions and needs assessor, a role which continued throughout the workshop. Had there been a satisfactory balance between freedom and structure at this more detailed level?

In each role the leader had to constantly weigh up variables which she saw as relevant to a situation and then decide how to proceed. This was not always easy. Her role as facilitator during discussions provides some examples. When the subject matter was wide-ranging, the leader found herself debating when to gather together points in order to help students who appeared to be a little confused, and when not to do so because there was a risk of breaking the momentum of a discussion and possibly bringing it to a premature halt, which would not be helpful to those whose thoughts were running ahead of the others. Also sometimes during the course of a discussion she had to make up her mind whether to introduce theoretical explanations, or whether for the time being to refrain because the students were grappling with enough new ideas. At other times, she had to judge whether it would be helpful to draw the attention of particular students to their apparent tendency to identify strongly with some of the clients whom they were discussing, or whether to trust them to make connections for themselves. The leader thought it important that the students should be able to discuss matters of particular importance to them, but sometimes a discussion went off at a tangent as a way of avoiding issues which the students found difficult, for example, after the role-play on the second morning of the first workshop. The leader then had to decide whether or not to redirect the discussion. On occasion she did seek to push the discussion in a particular direction, especially if it seemed likely it would lead to an exploration of general principles relevant to their future work in the community. For example, at the end of the first day (item 13), she encouraged the students to think around two topics which they raised in the course of discussion, that is, giving clients sufficient opportunity to express themselves and how the difficulties experienced by a client may trigger off strong personal feelings in a helper.

The less tight the structure of a workshop the more the leader has to make decisions on the spot. Sometimes the most appropriate ones may not be made, but an advantage of freedom is that it may well be possible to rectify this during the workshop. It is, however, important for a leader to reflect afterwards on how personal style of decision-making might perhaps be modified and whether an event has generated any new ideas which might be pursued. On this occasion, for instance, the leader wondered whether it would have helped at least some of the students to draw rather more attention to themes running through the workshop which provided underlying links between items; threads can be lost and the whole episode seem somewhat confusing to a student who is coping not only with new knowledge but also with new learning processes. It might perhaps also be helpful on occasion to comment to the students rather more while the workshop was actually running about why this or that decision on how to run it was being made and the choices which were open. This type of self-disclosure can be a useful way of encouraging the students to think about the criteria they themselves use when they are interviewing clients.

Sometimes when looking back on a workshop it can be all too easy to be self-critical. In retrospect it may seem 'obvious' that a better course of action would have been this or that because a particular situation is now being viewed rather differently, although it cannot be known with any certainty what would have been the outcome had the decisions been other than those which were made. Thinking around an event and recognising alternative courses of action which may perhaps not have been seen at the time, can, however, be an effective way to learn if the process is used constructively as a means for increasing resources by becoming alert to alternative ways of coping.

SOME CONCLUDING COMMENTS

The topic of this chapter has been the process of planning, running and assessing workshops and the theme has been the leader as learner. The leader's decision-making before and during the workshops was influenced by factors with their roots in herself, her resources, knowledge, beliefs, assumptions, skills, past experiences, in other people, such as the needs of the students as she interpreted them, both as adult learners and as nurses training to be health visitors, and in constraints from outside, such as place of meeting and time available.

Uncertainties are an inherent feature of running workshops and particularly so if the leader decides against a rigid structure. Most workshops are run to give those who attend an opportunity to learn about themselves, about other people, about how to fulfil particular roles in life etc. On the day the leader can never know with certainty how successful or otherwise a workshop is for the participants. Learning carries risks and involves change and may be associated with a whole gamut of emotions, and people change in different ways and at different rates and not everyone in a particular workshop is going to change. It is not often that a leader can follow up participants after the event to find out if attending has proved useful to them in the longer term. The students after the first workshop described steps they were going to take as a result of attending the workshop, but the leader was unlikely ever to know what they actually did after they had walked out of the door. The most a leader can do is to offer opportunities for learning and trust group members to use those opportunities if they find they are appropriate for them.

But the leader has some control over personal learning. The leader can choose whether or not to use the experience of running a workshop as an opportunity for rethinking and for increasing personal resources. This demands effort before, during, and after the event, over and above that of actually planning and running a workshop. And running workshops is hard work. Besides the preparation, it requires continuous concentration while the workshop is in progress in order to gather information, weigh it up and make decisions; it needs a range of resources which can be applied flexibly, a capacity to tolerate uncertainty and a willingness to commit oneself to the task as a whole person. It is suggested that these are all important attributes of the leader as learner, although not necessarily the only ones and no attempt has been made to assess priorities.

If it is such hard work for a leader-learner to run workshops, then why do it? In spite of all the difficulties, there are those who continue to play the game. They may perhaps do it for the money (if there is any); they may do it for altruistic reasons because they want to help others to help themselves more effectively; or their main aim may be to add to their own experiences and knowledge and skills. In addition, however, the chances are that they also do it because they find it helps to satisfy needs within themselves. They like to savour the subtleties of the game and the challenge to go on and face the pleasures and rewards, uncertainties and pain associated with learning and facilitating learning. It is hard work, it can be very uncomfortable, yet there are those who carry on leading again and again!

APPENDIX

| Stage | Topic | Type Of Exercise | Details |
|---|---|---|---|
| 1 Getting down to work | 1 General introduction | Brief talk by leader | General introduction to the workshop |
| | 2 Warm-up exercise | Group exercise | Getting to know each other; give christian name and adjective with same initial letter; throw cushion to indic- ate next speaker |
| | 3 Non-verbal communica- tion: feelings | Group exercise | In circle, each person acts emotion and others guess what it is |
| | 4 Non-verbal communica- tion: body language | a) Exercise in pairs b) Group discussion | Each pair given list of exercises on body and seating positions |
| | 5 Coffee | General chat | |
| | 6 Non-verbal communica- tion: uniforms | Group discussion | |
| | | ------------- | |
| 2 Increa- sing challenge of the learning process | 7 Listening & summarising | a) Exercise in pairs b) Group discussion | One person describes case for 5 minutes; partner listens, then summarises and comments on verbal & non-verbal communication; check for accuracy. Reverse roles |
| | 8 Lunch | Individual arrangements | |
| | 9 Warm-up exercise | Group exercise | 'Mixed Veg' (for des- cription see chapter 2) |

Training Student Health Visitors in Helping Skills

| Stage | Topic | Type Of Exercise | Details |
|---|---|---|---|
| | 10 Questioning | a) Group exercise <br> b) Group discussion | Role-play by two group members |
| | 11 Talking about feelings | a) Individual exercise <br><br> b) Discussion in two groups <br> c) Group discussion | Completion of charts describing degrees of intensity of certain feelings <br> Aim: reach consensus on how to complete charts <br> Comparison of results |
| | 12 Tea | General chat | |
| | 13 Initial interviews | a) Listening to recorded extracts from two tapes <br> b) Group discussions | Extracts from two interviews with different patterns of client/counsellor interactions |

------------

| 3 Resuming the task | 14 Venues for workshop | Group discussion | Discussion arising from interruption to item 9 |
| | 15 Warm-up exercise | Group exercise | The 'Knot' (see foot of table for description) |
| | 16 Empathic responding | a) Individual exercise <br> b) Group discussion | Rating of counsellors' responses to statements by clients |
| | 17 Coffee | General chat | |

------------

| 4 Role-play | 18 The health visitor & her clients: | a) Two role-playing exercises | Two visitors to the workshop played the role of clients in two different situations; |

107

Training Student Health Visitors in Helping Skills

| Stage | Topic | Type Of Exercise | Details |
|---|---|---|---|
| 4 cont. | 18 Initial visits | b) Group discussion | two students played the role of health visitors |
| | | ---------- | |
| 5 Interlude | 19 Lunch | General chat | |
| | 20 Warm-up exercise | Group exercise | The 'Knot' (see below) |
| | | ---------- | |
| 6 Assessment & evaluation | 21 Learning in the workshop: assessment | a) Individual exercise b) Group discussion | Self-evaluation of communication skills |
| | 22 Tea | General chat | |
| | 23 Building on the workshop experience | Individual exercises | Each student wrote a letter to herself beginning: 'As a result of this workshop, I will........' |
| | 24 Future workshops | Group discussion | Suggestions for workshops for the next group of student health visitors |
| | | ---------- | |

The 'Knot'
All participants join hands in a line; first person weaves in and out of the line and round in circles, then joins hands with last person so that line has now become a complicated knot; the task of the group is to untie themselves from the knot without anyone letting go of the hand of the person on each side and to finish up facing inwards holding hands in a circle.

REFERENCES

Argyle, M. (ed) (1981) Social Skills and Health, Methuen, London
Belle, D. (1982) 'The Stress of Caring: Women as Providers of of Social Support', in Goldberger, Leo and Breznitz,

Schlomo (eds), Handbook of Stress: Theoretical and
Clinical Aspects, Free Press, New York

Bridge, W. and Clark, J.M. (eds) (1981) Communication in
Nursing Care, H.M. and M. Publishers, London

Carkhuff, R.R. and Berenson, B.G. (1977) Beyond Counselling and
Therapy, 2nd edit., Holt, Rinehart and Winston, New York

Counselling in Nursing, (1978) Report of a Working Party held
under the auspices of the RCN Institute of Advanced
Nursing Education, Royal College of Nursing, London

Freire, P. (1972) Pedagogy of the Oppressed, Penguin,
Harmondsworth

Holmberg, B. (1984) Adult Education: Students' Independence and
Autonomy as Foundations and as Educational Outcomes, Ziff
Popiere 49, Fern Universitat, Haghn

Hopson, B. (1982) 'Counselling and Helping', in Hall, J. (ed),
Psychology for Nurses and Health Visitors, The British
Psychological Society and MacMillan, London

James, N. (1984) 'A Postscript to Nursing', in Bell, C. and
Roberts, H. (eds), Social Researching: Politics, Problems
and Practice, Routledge and Kegan Paul, London

Jaques, D. (1984) Learning in Groups, Croom Helm, London

Knowles, M.S. (1970) The Modern Practice of Adult Education,
Association Press, New York

Lindblom, C. (1986) The Policy Making Process, Prentice-Hall,
Englewood Cliffs

McIntosh, J. (1981) 'Communicating with Patients in their own
Homes  in Bridge W. and Clark, J.M. (eds), Communication
in Nursing Care, H.M. and M. Publishers, London

Marton, F. and Saljo, R. (1984) 'Approaches to Learning', in
Marton, F., Hounsell, D. and Entwistle, N. (eds), The
Experience of Learning, Scottish Academic Press, Edinburgh

Maslow, A.H. (1970) Motivation and Personality, 2nd edit.,
Harper and Row, New York

Mezirow, J. (1981) 'A Critical Theory of Adult Learning and
Education', Adult Education, 32, No. 1, pp. 3-24

More, W.S. (1974) Emotions and Adult Learning, Gower Publishing
Co., Farnborough

Nelson-Jones, R. (1982) The Theory and Practice of Counselling
Psychology, Holt, Rinehart and Winston, London

Nelson-Jones, R. (1983) Practical Counselling Skills, Holt,
Rinehart and Winston, London[1]

Open University Course E355 (1984) Educating Adults, The Open
University Press, Milton Keynes

Palozzoli, M.S., Boscolo, L., Cecchin, G. and Prata, G. (1978)
Paradox and Counter-Paradox, Jason Aronson, London

Parkes, C.M. (1972) Bereavement: Studies of Grief in Adult
Life, Penguin, Harmondsworth

[1]A number of the ideas for practical exercises used in the
workshops described in this chapter were adapted from suggestions in Nelson-Jones (1983).

Perry, W.G. (1970) Forms of Intellectual and Ethical
    Development in the College Years: A Scheme, Holt,
    Rinehart and Winston, New York
Proctor, B. (1978) Counselling Shop, Burnett Books, London
Rogers, C.R. (1957) 'The Necessary and Sufficient Conditions of
    Therapeutic Personality Change', Journal of Consulting
    Psychology, 21, pp. 95-104
Rogers, C.R. (1969) Freedom to Learn, Merrill, Columbus, Ohio
Rogers, C.R. (1984) Freedom to Learn for the '80's, Merrill,
    Columbus, Ohio
Schon, D. (1983) The Reflective Practitioner: How Professionals
    Think in Action, Temple Smith, London
Stockwell, F. (1972) The Unpopular Patient, Royal College of
    Nursing, London
Svensson, L. (1984) 'Skill in Learning', in Marton, F.,
    Hounsell, D. and Entwistle, N. (eds), The Experience of
    Learning, Scottish Academic Press, Edinburgh
A Systematic Approach to Nursing Care: An Introduction,(1984),
    Open University Course P553, Open University Press,
    Milton Keynes
Tough, A. (1976) 'Self-Planned Learning and Major Personal
    Change', in Smith, R.M. (ed), Adult Learning: Issues and
    Innovation, ERIC Clearing House in Career Education,
    Northern Illinois University
Van der Molen, P.P. (1985) 'Learning Self-Actualisation and
    Psychotherapy', in Apter, M.J., Fontana, D. and
    Murgatroyd, S. (eds), Reversal Theory: Applications and
    Developments, University College Cardiff Press, Cardiff
Woolfe, R. and Murgatroyd, S. (1979) 'The Open University and
    the Negotiation of Knowledge', Higher Education Review,
    11, No. 2, pp. 9-16
Wattley, L.A. and Muller, D.J. (1984) Investigating Psychology:
    A Practical Approach for Nursing, Harper and Row, London
'Working Party on Management Structure in the Local Authority
    Nursing Service' (Mayston), report published in 1969, and
    referred to in A Discussion Document produced by the
    Health Visitor Advisory Group of the Royal College of
    Nursing Society of Primary Health Care Nursing, (1984),
    Royal College of Nursing, London

Chapter Six

COPING WITH DEATH : WORKSHOPS FOR THOSE HELPING WITH THE DYING
AND BEREAVED

MIKE SHOOTER

Any group setting out to offer a workshop experience for those
helping with the dying and bereaved has two questions to ask of
itself: why choose such a well-trodden field as death education
and why in a workshop?
     It is our contention that the answers to both questions
are the same. It is not the words of counsellors that help
most, but the outlet they offer for their clients' grief; and
so it is with the counsellors themselves. They do not require
yet more words of advice, but an opportunity to express the
emotional pains of helping that might otherwise prevent their
knowledge being put into action. An experiential workshop
offers that opportunity.

CONTEXT : ACHIEVEMENTS AND NEEDS

Ten years ago, the Senior Editor of the American Medical
Association claimed that 'Dying is being worked to death'
(Vaisrub 1974). He felt himself submerged in a tide of essays,
editorials, books and journals on the subject of death and
dying, overflowing from the medical into lay literature and
the mass media. The tide has continued to run - to scan the
medical and sociological shelves in any bookshop is to be aware
that for the aspiring author there is more life in death than
any other subject!

The Growth Of Knowledge: The 'Normal' Framework
Clearly, knowledge of the phenomena of death and mourning are
essential. For clients and helpers alike, one of the greatest
fears is of unleashing a boundless chaos of emotions against
which the only defence is to keep all feeling firmly battened
down. It is true that 'death always comes wreathed in culture'
(Porter 1981) and that personality variation means there is no
one way of helping the dying (Stedeford 1979); but the experience accumulated and communicated by experts lays down landmarks in the chaos by which 'normal' may be distinguished from
'abnormal' and the paths of intervention planned.

111

It has taken medicine 400 years to agree with Shakespeare
that the expression of grief is healing in itself for patient
and doctor alike (Macbeth IV, iii, 209; British Medical Journal
1980: 'give sorrow words') but the lesson is a good one nonetheless. The grief cycle, its stages and the emotions appropriate to them have been clearly set out from Freud (1917) to
Kubler-Ross (1969). The child's conception of death has been
re-examined and a path opened through a thicket of misguided
protection for children once more to share in the process of
mourning. Death has been re-framed as a family affair (Pincus
1917). The need for grieving has been recognised in areas like
stillbirths (Lewis 1979) where it had hitherto been swept under
a carpet of encouragement to get on with life - although it
does not seem to have been extended to the 'hidden grief' of
miscarriage (Oakley 1984). The concept of mourning has spread
for the first time to the analogous separations of divorce,
handicap, amputation and even unemployment (Murgatroyd and
Shooter 1983).

## Practical Skills: Development Of Counselling
Upon this knowledge has been built the basic skills of bereavement counselling, the arts of establishing a trusting relationship, of working through grief with the client and of withdrawing without compounding the loss. And upon such skills are
created systems of help offered by professional services and
'expert' support, voluntary services like Cruse staffed by
trained volunteers guided by professionals, and self-help
groups of the bereaved like the League of Compassionate Friends
bringing help to others in similar situations, (Parkes 1980).
Some at least of these services have been tested and shown to
'work' (Raphael 1971).

## The Gap Between Words And Practice
And yet, despite all this accumulated knowledge about death,
dying and how to help, there still seems to be a huge gap
between words and practice. All the knowledge accumulated and
the counselling skills developed, all the encouragement towards
open expression and the sharing of grief, has failed to
counteract the increasing 'sanitisation' of death in the modern
age.
    Ironically, medicine's obsession with the preservation of
life has transferred the setting of death from the family bedroom to the hospital ward - or, more often, to a screened-off
cubicle as far from the sight of others as possible. The morgue
in the hospital basement has taken the place of the front-room
parlour as a resting-place for the body. Children are seldom
present at the death, often prevented from visiting before
death and rarely get the chance to say 'goodbye' after death.
As the very sight of death is removed from the home, so it has
ceased to be part of a child's or anyone else's familiar education. With this and the widespread breakdown of religion and

a belief in the afterlife, death has become increasingly feared and decreasingly talked about.

In 1980, the London Medical Group could still call its conference 'Death: the last Taboo'. Even in the United States, where the need for death education 'in a death-denying society' (Crase and Crase 1974) has led to its introduction into the school curriculum in many areas, it is done in haphazard fashion with no disciplines accepting responsibility for training and proficiency of the educators. The individual teacher is left to struggle through the death of a pupil and its effects on his classmates by his own compassion and insight (Evans 1982).

Medicine both reflects and reinforces the general taboo. Death education in the United States was only 'slightly more integrated into the medical school curriculum' in 1980 than it was in 1975 (Dickinson 1981) and 80% of it was limited to occasional lectures and short 'mini-courses'. In Britain, general practitioners regret the woeful lack of training at postgraduate level (Keane 1983). For the hospital houseman, his emergence from behind the screens on the first night of casualty duty will be the first time he has had to tell a waiting relative of their loved-one's death and the first time he has had to face the meaning of death in his medical career; consultants will continue to pass the buck to their juniors, hiding their own tears behind the assertion that these things can only be learnt by experience.

Few nursing schools offer training in caring for the dying (Hopping 1977); in at least one major teaching hospital in the last year, the inadequate seminars that did exist were threatened under the financial cutbacks on the premise that it was the most expendable part of the course! Most social workers and health visitors with dying and bereaved clients work alone with little guidance and less opportunity for emotional support.

## Inter-Agency Confusion: The Lack Of Communication
Since a number of caring agencies are likely to be involved with the dying and bereaved at any one time, knowledge is essential in another way too - the knowledge of what each of those agencies is saying and doing so that they may work as a co-ordinated network to help their clients and not distress them further by pulling in opposite emotional and practical directions. And again that knowledge goes unheeded; the literature is full of battles over policy between nursing and medical staff in hospitals leading at best to passive paralysis and at worst to an active fight over the prostrate patient in the ward (Andrews 1974). A woman talks of being visited at home by a health visitor for the 'first post-natal check' - except that no-one at the hospital had bothered to inform the health visitor that the baby had been miscarried! (Oakley 1984).

It is no one's responsibility discreetly to tell a child's teacher of a death in the family, and yet close parent/school co-operation is essential if he is to be sensitive to the grief

that can so dramatically alter the behaviour of the child and
his classmates (Fredlund 1977).

## Clients As The Sufferers: The Loneliness Of Death
Not suprisingly, the ultimate sufferers are the clients themselves. While the lucky few die in an open, warm and supportive home atmosphere, the image in the modern age is of 'The
Invisible Death' (Aries 1981) in which dying has been stifled
by medical routine in the loneliness of the terminal ward where
people no longer even 'know' they are dying and the dying are
corralled off from the living in a 'conspiracy of silence'
(Knight and Field 1981). Nurses and doctors fight for the right
to give a patient death with dignity or the horrors of repeated,
last-ditch resuscitation. Even the hospice movement, magnific-
ent as its conception may have been in its family approach
(Saunders 1972) is seen by many as yet another way of tucking
death away into a corner of society where none of us need be
aware it's there.

Ten years after Vaisrub's editorial, the Ombudsman's
attention was still being drawn to hospitals' failure to handle
bereaved relatives appropriately. His repeated calls for action
on their behalf (Annual Reports of the Health Service Commissioner, 1980-81, 1981-82, 1983-84) have finally prompted a draft
Department of Health and Social Security circular to all Health
Authorities. It is welcome in itself, but since the Ombudsman
was neither consulted nor informed of its issue, any pessimism
about its likely effect seems wholly justified!

Perhaps Vaisrub, in one way, was right. 'It is too easy to
write about death'; it is much more difficult for those words
to take effect. Why then has there been such a gap between our
knowledge of the dying process and how best to help on the one
hand and the implementation of that knowledge in everyday practice on the other; and how might a workshop be best designed to
fill it?

## AIMS AND THEIR RATIONALE : WHY THE NEEDS REMAIN

## Recognition Of The Helpers' Feelings
Our workshops have been founded on the assertion that helping
in any way with the dying and bereaved is emotionally 'painful'
and that the behaviour of helpers, no matter what their intentions, is subject to the same defences against that pain as
those they are trying to help.

Fear of being overwhelmed. The dying patient demands an intensity of communication that can feel overwhelming to relative
and helper alike. It 'can invoke the fear of being drawn into
the dying process itself' (Hagglund 1981). There can sometimes
seem no half-way house between being absorbed into a mother-
infant symbiosis of total dependency or avoiding contact
altogether.

114

Our own death anxieties. Helping the bereaved inevitably
arouses the fears of our own death that we all carry within us.
The need to repress those fears is so great that over half
general practitioners questioned denied that they existed or
made counselling the dying difficult! (Keane 1982). It may
awaken memories of actual bereavements in the life of the
helper; a therapist may even be bereaved during the course of
therapy itself. The therapist may be faced with walking a
tightrope between helping his own grief through the client and
denying the client any share of his own loss at all. How
successfully he walks that tightrope towards an appropriate
sharing that can increase awareness of client needs will determine whether the helper merely re-enacts pathological responses in the client's family or offers a model for healthy
resolution (Givelbar and Simon 1981).

The sense of failure. For those trained in preventing illness,
healing the sick and prolonging life, the death of a client
can mean a loss of self-esteem and a sense of failure founded
on the fallacy that the only true hope that can be given is
cure rather than helping with the dying process itself. Once
the client is consigned to the inevitable, 'it is not surprising to find the physician hurrying away from the scene to deal
with other patients who are not dying but recovering and with
whom he can regain lost composure and a sense of accomplish-
ment'. (Siver 1980). Where death is due to major disease it is
difficult enough but the helpers 'guilt' may be made part of a
corporate responsibility of medicine or assuaged by a sense of
the natural order. The 'failure' to carry a client through a
healthy process like pregnancy and childbirth means that stillbirth and miscarriage are particularly guilt ridden.

The death of a relationship. No matter how much the helper
struggles to retain a professional objectivity, a relationship
is built up with the dying and their relatives that cannot be
broken without it being a bereavement in itself. A patient
admitted repeatedly to hospital or visited at home over a long
period is to a helper 'no longer simply the woman in such-and-
such a room but the friend to whom she has listened, with whom
she has planned care, faced the pain of illness and hope for the
future'. (Sonstegard 1976). The death of a client is a death
for the helper and helped alike.

## How Feelings Interfere With Practice

Mutual defences. Distress, therefore, may actually be more
severe among care-givers than patients; care-givers may go
through exactly the same grief-cycle with all its stages and
attendant emotions of anger, guilt and misery as the bereaved
- and against them they may marshal the same defences. 'There
is no reaction among patients that cannot also occur in

care-givers'. (Weisman 1981).

Some of these defences may be necessary to professional survival but the danger is that the care-giver's struggle with his own feelings becomes not simply a reflection but a reinforcement of that of the client. Defences of care-giver and cared -for become inextricably linked.

Suppression of information. Thus, for example, it is clearly established that sharing knowledge of prognosis between the dying and their relatives draws them closer together in their grieving but that this conflicts with a natural desire in the survivors to protect themselves and the dying from the emotional pain of it. The model for good sharing that they need comes from the professionals involved in their care. Hinton(1981) has shown how 'a unit where people are quite prepared to speak honestly and openly with the dying had more of their patients embarking on a similar dialogue with their wife or husband'. But repressing pain by repressing information is all too common and in the process interferes with honest inter-personal relationships within the family. The medics' need to protect themselves, albeit couched in a need to protect their patients, 'destroys the mutual confidence between husband and wife..... that must remain intact and grow during this trying period'. (Silver 1980).

Tailoring what is said. Many carers claim to 'tailor' what they say to the dying and bereaved, according to the strengths and weaknesses of the people concerned. 'What one tells a patient requires individualisation and medical art'. (Silver 1980). But, 'it would be a brave and probably inexperienced man who claims to assess this factor with confidence'. (British Medical Journal 1974). It often results in 'little more than an inconsistent ad hoc practice evolving from the early example of their tutors followed by the accretion of troubled memories, avoided embarrassments, deferred decisions and the encouragement of those who have died well!'. Past surveys have shown that surgeons tell roughly the same thing to everybody, and that is very little (McGuire 1975). When they do make distinctions according to what they deem to be patient vulnerabilities, they are notoriously prone to get it wrong.

Such may be the vulnerability of the carers and their need to defend themselves against their own distress, that the suspicion grows that the dying - (of whom far more know their prognosis than staff would imagine [Hinton 1980]) actually tailor what they discuss to the character of the carer rather than the other way around! The end result may be a loneliness of grieving with staff, patient and relatives isolated in their wish to protect themselves and the others from the pain they would so much more constructively share. The author has known doctors, nurses, the social worker and the health visitor, all aware of a particular client's diagnosis and unable to discuss

it, while the dying client, his spouse and his children retired
separately to the same attic bedroom at different times to cry
alone lest they damage the others: carers and cared-for divided
by knowledge rather than united by it in their grief.

## How The Workshop Might Help

How could we help? How could we lower those inappropriately
erected defences that 'cause more suffering than any other
problem except unrelieved pain'? (Stedeford 1981). Stedeford
believes that it is the easiest problem to treat because the
answer lies within ourselves as carers rather than those we
are trying to help but that, of course, is the very nub of the
problem. In order to come to terms with their own feelings,
carers need as much emotional support as they give to those in
their charge. The National Organiser of Cruse has appealed for
us to 'accept our need of help no matter what our profession
or status within it'. (Nuttall 1977). His call for bereavement
counselling in the training of carers to be followed by support
groups for all those working with bereavement has been echoed
in hospitals, schools and community; but such are the depths of
the defences involved in trainers and helpers that any forum
that does exist is still lecture based. Most workers with the
dying do so without emotional support. Few services see that
the 'plight of the caregivers' (Weisman 1981) is as valid as
the distress they are trying to resolve.

Our workshops are aimed to do just that in providing an
opportunity for carers from all walks of life to share their
feelings within safe boundaries. By doing so, we do not set
out to decrease the death anxieties of those involved. Too
many studies have set out to evaluate the impact of bereavement
training in just such terms and with inevitably equivocal results (McClam 1980). This seems to us as misguided a view of the
needs of the carers as those who, in turn, criticise the concept of the grief cycle for not decreasing the pain of death
for the dying and bereaved. What our workshops are designed to
do is to provide an outlet for those feelings and, therefore,
to stop the need to repress them otherwise interfering in the
quality of care. Only by facing up to our feelings as carers
can we encourage those we are trying to help to do likewise.
As with the dying and bereaved themselves, what the carers
need and what we have set out to provide, is not more words
but listening - a listening to painful feelings and offering
a chance to share them with others in mutual support.

The following is an account of the experiences of the
Open University Coping With Crisis group in running such workshops over the past two years and of the author's use of modified versions of the workshops in a variety of contexts.

Coping with Death: Helping the Dying and Bereaved

FORMAT : PRINCIPLES AND STRUCTURES

Principles

The workshop leaders. The Coping With Crisis and Training Group,
under whose aegis the workshops have been run, is drawn from a
wide variety of professions with a common commitment to working
with people in life crises, including bereavement. One of the
expressed aims behind the formation of the group was the
sharing of problems between people of overlapping fields of
work but whose angle of approach was different enough to provoke new ideas; nowhere does that seem more vital than in
bereavement. Death education is still dominated by physicians
(especially psychiatrists) and theologians (Dickinson 1981). It
would be begging the question to say the least to expect two
professions about whose attitudes much concern has been expressed to instill a more insightful approach! The composition of
the training group reflects the social network of different
agencies helping with the dying and bereaved in co-operation
rather than one stereotyped view.

The participants. For the same reasons, our initial aim was to
open each workshop to all those working with the dying and
bereaved in any way instead of offering separate workshops to
different groups of workers in turn. Duncombe (1974) has
stressed how discussion is enhanced in a multidisciplinary
setting. We hoped, in addition to personal growth, to foster
links between people appreciating for the first time the particular problems confronting those in other professions rather
than carping at each other from rival ivory towers. The workshops are, therefore, advertised by a comprehensive mailing
list and by posters and leaflets in hospitals, health centres,
child guidance clinics, schools, social services headquarters,
university and local government offices. Acceptance was so
arranged as to ensure a good mix rather than on a first-come-
first-served basis. The workshops would be about sharing in all
senses of the word.

The importance of boundaries: size, timing and setting. In any
group activity designed to encourage its participants to expose
painful, hitherto well defended feelings, 'boundaries' are
clearly important and we have given considerable thought to
the size of the group, the length of the workshop and the
building in which they have been run. The exercises involved
(see below) require an ideal of around twelve people. This has
meant running the workshops more often than we had envisaged to
satisfy the demand, but the rewards of retaining an intimate
small-group atmosphere have been great. We have occasionally
given in to pressure and doubled the number, but this then
becomes a large group with all its attendant problems and the
potentially greater cross current of experiences and opinion

118

has been stemmed by the need to divide into smaller sub-groups within the workshop to retain any sense of 'safety'.

Each workshop so far has been for one day only with two, three-hour, morning and afternoon sessions and a break for lunch that itself has usually been a communal activity, but in which the participants have been allowed to 'escape' if they felt the need for privacy. We have found empirically that this structure gives us the time and continuity to facilitate emotional expression without the threat of things 'going on forever'. In other words, our aim has been to promote a good experience of sharing within safe boundaries that the particip- ants may then carry over into their lives outside the work- shop. We have not claimed to resolve all the feelings provoked within the day itself, nor would that seem appropriate.

We have used a building that has a large enough space for whole-group discussion and a number of separate rooms for smaller group activities where appropriate. It is easily accessible, free from interruption, and is non-hospital, non- educational, non-religious, 'neutral' territory. To say that it is warm and comfortable sounds prosaic, but anyone who has tried to run workshops in cold, barren barns will appreciate the links between physical and emotional 'climate'! Perhaps we have been lucky with the resources at our disposal but it is really not that difficult to do better than the rushed, sporadic, over-large and formalised seminars run in lecture halls and anatomy dissection rooms that have passed for 'work- shops' elsewhere! (Marks and Bertman 1980).

Experiential nature: for participants and group leaders. Within these boundaries, our emphasis has been on as experiential a programme as possible. Only by actively challenging people at an emotional level can significant changes be expected (Durlak 1978). That being so, it has been important to make sure that all those applying for the workshop have a clear idea of what they might be expected to contribute. Each workshop has been accompanied by a carefully worded leaflet distributed with the publicity.

One of the clearest messages to those who come to the workshop is that it is impossible to help with the dying and bereaved successfully by remaining professionally detached and aloof; the helpers must share in the pain. And the same is true of helping the helpers - it is important for the organisers of the workshop to set the model by fully participating in the experiences of the day. This is made easier by different mem- bers of the group being responsible for different sections of the day, freeing the rest. One member of the group, in rotation, attends each workshop solely as a 'consumer'.

Structure and flexibility: responding to the moment. How can we 'plan' for spontaneous experience? Clearly the workshop needs to have some sort of loose structure for members to hold

onto in exactly the same way that helping the dying and bereaved needs a sense of the normal landmarks of grieving. Within
that, it needs the flexibility to respond to the immediate
needs of individuals and the group as a whole as they arise.
This means interspersing the exercises with discussion periods;
talking and listening to the feelings around is as important as
the exercises provoking and carrying them, just as the sharing
of the feelings of grief are as important as the rituals of
funeral and burial that are a vehicle for them. It may mean
amplifying an exercise by another if necessary (e.g. sculpting
relationships emerging from a role-play) or spending double
the amount of time on one bit of the day at the expense of a
'favourite' exercise the organisers had planned for later! It
may mean altering the whole course of the day to suit the
circumstances. And it will always mean responding not only to
group 'temperature' but watching carefully throughout for the
reactions of each individual. No two people will react the
same. We start with different backgrounds and different vulnerabilities; one individual will sail through an exercise that
another will find devastating. People will get upset during
the course of the day; we are dealing with upsetting feelings.
But the organisers need to be sensitive enough to individual
casualties, to help them begin to work through that upset and
to emerge from the day with enough strengths to carry on working with those feelings when everyone has gone home and they do
not have the sustaining intimacy of the group around them.

General Structure
The structure of our workshop has changed significantly over
the two or more years we have been running them. Our original
'plan' divided the time roughly equally between a three-hour
morning session devoted to invoking the feelings involved in a
variety of bereavement situations and a three-hour afternoon
session looking at the problems they present to us as professionals working simultaneously with those feelings inside ourselves and the clients we try to help. The afternoon session
was greatly changed in later workshops.
    Both sessions are prefaced by 'warm-up' exercises - in
the morning to break the ice of unfamiliarity in a group that
may contain one or two people who have met before but who are
otherwise strangers to each other; in the afternoon to get
people moving again both physically and emotionally after the
necessary 'let down' of lunch.

Morning Session - Role Playing Of Common Bereavement Situations
The value of role-play in 'death education' has been well doc-
umented (Barton 1975). Inevitably it meets with some resistance
in a group of widely different familiarity with active techniques and the danger is to try and cope with that by a long
period of explanation and reassurance. In our experience this
does little more than give people longer to get nervous! There

is no better way of coping with resistance than by getting on
with it as soon as possible.

Preparation for the role-plays. The large group divides into
two, three or four sub-groups according to numbers (each role-
play requires five or six participants) and are led to separate
rooms with two organisers per sub-group. There the participants
are randomly handed a 'script' each for one of the roles that
gives them a brief description of themselves and their attitudes, the other family or community members, the general situation facing them all and an immediate 'flash-point'. This is
not meant as a film-script to be followed to the letter but as
a framework which the role-player will spontaneously begin to
fill in from the fabric of personal experience in his own
family and those he has tried to help. In the process, the
role-play becomes a powerful vehicle for feelings thus made
accessible for working through in the rest of the day.

By the law of numbers, some female roles will have to be
played by men and vice-versa; adults will have to play children
and single people play parents. This is not an inconvenience.
At the very least it is a challenge to accepted roles; at best
it arouses previously repressed memories or first insights into
problems a helper may have failed to appreciate in people whose
responsibilities they have never experienced themselves.

Examples of role-play scenarios. 1. A mother returns from
hospital where her husband is dying from injuries received in
a road crash. She is faced with the decision of how to break
the news to her children and whether to allow them to visit
him. The youngest child, a boy of seven, has always had difficulty separating from mother; the eldest nine, has always
been 'daddy's girl'. The children's grandmother, who lost her
own husband a few years ago and has bottled up her grief, is
concerned to spare the children 'any upset'. Their father's
sister knows he was probably drunk again. She feels he has a
right to see the children. Her husband wouldn't want anyone to
see him looking like that.....
2. The 40 year old managing director of a firm, who has been
working flat out to prevent it going bust, has been told by
his friend and G.P. that he has inoperable cancer and will
probably die in about a year. Gradually losing touch with his
wife because of his work, he can't share this with her at all.
Panic-stricken by her prompting, he begins to hit her around.
His eldest son's exam work has begun to suffer as he feels
himself responsible for sorting things out. His daughter thinks
her father is going mad and accuses her mother of driving him
to it. The G.P. feels a failure at not being able to cure his
friend. His doubts about the wisdom of telling him the truth
are not helped by his own wife, who tried to persuade him not
to from the start. The managing director attacks his wife, who
rings in desperation for the friends to come around and rescue

121

her.....

3. A young, single girl, whose illegitimate spina bifida baby died at six weeks old, feels the baby was punished for her own sins. She refused to go to the funeral, had not been to see her in the hospital and does not recognise her death in any way. She has gone back to live with her alcoholic, divorced mother who clings onto her 'baby', in the same way her daughter clings onto the idea of her's. The girl has become agoraphobic despite the attempts of her father to get her out and about. A younger brother was once close to her but cannot understand her attitude now. Father invites her elder sister to come round with her own, new-born, healthy baby to 'snap her out of it'. The sister's husband, who comes too, is not at all sure it was a good idea.....

4. The father of a four year old boy, twice operated on unsuccessfully and now dying at home of cardiac defects, is so devastated that he forbids talk of it with his wife, let alone with the son himself or his two older daughters. The eldest daughter is brittly bright. The youngest daughter carries the guilt of her brother's sudden relapse on the one occasion she was allowed to visit him in hospital, the more so since she resented the attention he got and had sometimes secretly wished him dead. She has now become anorexic (mimicking the way her brother vomited after feeds when he was a baby). Once again there has been a battle over a meal. Her mother wants her referred for help. But her husband would never allow it.....

5. The sudden death has just occurred of a grandmother who was the pillar of her family upon whom everyone leant for support. Unable to accept being progressively crippled with rheumatoid arthritis she took an overdose of pain-killers and sleeping tablets. Her 'child-like' husband has been told it was accidental. Her son, already guilty because of long periods spent away in Saudi Arabia, feels it must have been suicide and wants it hushed up. His depressive wife, alternately grateful to her mother-in-law for helping with the kids and angry that she did it so well, wants things opened up to get back at her husband for 'deserting' her. Her eldest son is busy denying his grandmother's death means anything to him. The youngest son, who was very close to his grandmother, is on his way home from school and will be calling in on her as usual. Who is going to tell him, what and how.....

After five minutes or so the scripts are retrieved by the organiser/observers and the role-play initiated at the flash point involved. (It is important to collect the scripts. Some of the more anxious participants, who might otherwise discover surprising spontaneity within themselves, cling to them like drowning men to wreckage!!). The role-play is left to run for upwards of half an hour - contrary to the participants' expectations, this never seems long enough. It does not have to come to any particular resolution, or any resolution at all. Real life is not so neatly packaged; there are no 'right' ways of doing it and no 'right' answers.

Building on the role-plays. We have found it valuable to have
an initial discussion of the role-play before de-roling so
that each character may explain to the others how it felt from
their point of view. They may be encouraged to illustrate this
further by the non-verbal exercise of 'sculpting' the relationships as they saw them, using the other bodies as clay to move
around nearer or farther from each other, looking away from or
towards each other, standing above one another or sitting below,
in front or behind, holding onto each other or pushing away. It
is surprising how the physical tensions created in the pieces
of the sculpture mirror the emotional tensions in the role-play
relationships. Some positions which prove impossible to maintain physically were 'impossible' emotionally too.

De-roling. The role-play is followed by an equally important
de-roling exercise. This may be as simple as each member rest-
ating their real name and occupation. They may then go on to
say how difficult or easy it was for them to 'play the role'
assigned to them, thus being given an opportunity to distance
themselves if they wish from anything they regarded as alien to
them. The participants need to stick with the feelings the
role-play has aroused, but not with the particular part they
have played, no matter how much of themselves it may have
contained.

Discussing the role-plays. After de-roling the members may
discuss how the characters they played related to their own
personal experiences. In our original workshops the sub-groups
gathered together again in the main room to do this. If the
role-plays had been the same scenario for each group, this had
the advantage of being able to compare the different ways the
same scripts had been played and to relate this to the different personal backgrounds of the players as an illustration of
how our conceptions of situations (and, therefore, of helping
the dying and bereaved) are moulded by the experiences of our
personal lives. Empirically, however, we have come to the
conclusion that this is out-weighed by the unwieldiness of the
larger group and subsequent workshops have stayed in the sub-
groups for all discussion of their role-plays. The players will
in any case share their experiences over lunch and this has
helped to maintain momentum and continuity between the morning
and afternoon sessions.

Role of the observers. Being an 'observer' in the role-plays
is not a sinecure or a simple distributer and collector of
scripts. Individual observers have played it many ways but it
is at any rate an active role. The observer may be required to
intervene if the role-play gets irretrievably stuck - and to
examine why it got stuck in terms of the 'stuck' feelings

involved. He or she must interpret the dynamics as they see
them and check them out with the individual players and the
group as a whole in the discussion period. It is important to
have two observers to each sub-group; observers themselves are
subjective and need to compare their observations with each
other as they go along. They need to rescue each other from a
sense of responsibility for how their sub-group's role-play
goes that might otherwise pressure them into intervening too
obtrusively. Their combined presence, however they may keep to
the background, serves to give the role-players a link with
reality and is an unconscious safety net around the emotions
released.

Reality and role-play: links and dilemmas. The material for
all of the role-plays has been culled from the author's case-
work, with the names and some details altered to preserve
confidentiality. In truth, they are such archetypal situations
that they are instantly 'recognisable' by anyone working with
the dying and bereaved. They will also come pretty close to
the personal experiences of some of the helpers; sooner or
later it is inevitable that one of the scenarios is a replica
of what a participant has gone or is going through. Since the
whole point of the workshops is to work with feelings rather
than avoid them, we would not generally think it appropriate
to 'tailor' the material to the particular members of a workshop even if our knowledge of the applicants' background was
good enough to allow it - we have criticised the medical
profession too hotly for doing that in the withholding of information from the dying and their relatives. But we did on one
occasion drop the fourth role-play (quoted above) when we
learnt at the start of the day that one of the members was
struggling with the recently diagnosed, inoperable heart-
failure of her young son. Whether we were right to do so is a
moot point. She had, after all, wanted to come to the workshop
and the general material of the day would in any case uncover
the feelings that were so close to the surface and which she
wanted to work on. But we decided that the particular role-play
was so 'close to the bone' that it allowed her no room for
emotional manoeuvre whatsoever. The author still has doubts
whether that decision was taken to protect here or to protect
ourselves and the rest of the group. It is possible that we
committed one of the errors we are trying to tackle in the
workshops, but we are human. Perhaps we should use that very
dilemma as a role-play in a subsequent workshop to think about
it further!

Afternoon Session

The original plan: inter-agency exercises. In the first few
workshops, the afternoon was designed to allow members to
retreat into their professional roles to examine how the

morning's feelings affect their attempts to help with the dying
and bereaved - and in the process to encourage appreciation of
the difficulties in professions other than their own.

Participants were paired with someone from the same or
analogous profession and asked to draw up a list of the
'strengths' and 'weaknesses' of members of a completely different profession in dealing with death. The lists were then
checked out with the self-conceptions of the other profession's
representatives in large group discussion afterwards. Not only
do professionals become aware of how little they know of other
agencies, but may sometimes come up with surprisingly keen
insights that the other agencies had been blind to in themselves. The whole group finished by working together on more
effective communication and co-ordination, as a reflection of
the inter-agency network necessary in work outside.

Later modifications: developing the feelings of the morning.
Latterly, however, the afternoon session has taken on a much
more experiential nature in line with the events of the morning.
The effect of the morning role-play proved so deep that we have
had to carve out further space in the afternoon to work on the
issues emerging from it; participants have found it impossible
to shift so suddenly (despite lunch intervening) from the
emotional to the intellectual plane.

Many of the participants will have been in touch not only
with experiences within their own families, but with anxieties
about their own death. The value of death-awareness exercises
has been noted elsewhere (Hammer 1971). We have built on this
by guided fantasy work in which the participants are asked to
spread out and put themselves into comfortable positions in
which they are further relaxed by typical relaxation techniques.
They are encouraged to fantasise on their own deaths and the
circumstances surrounding it: where it will take place, from
what cause, when, who will be present, whether it is a painful or painless experience, whether life is 'complete' or
whether there are regrets at things left undone, what things
need to be done, and so on. The participants are brought back
to the reality of the room at their own pace and instructed to
share their experience in pairs and large group discussion.

The links thus forged between the morning and afternoon
exercises and jobs outside the workshops, is no better illustrated than by the experience of one of the organisers attending the workshop as a consumer. His increasing difficulties
coping with a number of bereaved families in his job as a child
and family psychiatrist were highlighted by the morning role-
play in which the pain of playing a child with a dying parent
was intense. In the guided fantasy later, it became suddenly
clear for the first time that his death would be full of
regrets for the unresolved issues between himself and his
father that had remained repressed since adolescence. Following
the workshop he visited his father, about whom there were now

serious health worries, and was able to cross some of the
emotional and physical barriers that had divided them. Freed
from the personal defences it carried, his professional work
with the families in his care improved immediately.

The day has occasionally been ended by a set exercise like
the 'knot' in which the participants link hands in a chain, the
front person of which winds in and out of the rest, tying the
whole group in a tight heap which they must then disentangle by
their co-operative effort - thus symbolising the freeing of the
emotional knots that has been the main theme of the day.

More often, however, the members of a group between whom
there are now intimate bonds of trust and familiarity, come
together in a spontaneous physical and emotional huddle in the
centre of the room with each of them in turn, when ready, making a statement of what they have got from the day.

RESULTS

Size Of The Response
The workshops have had a large, continuing and wide-ranging
response - so much so that they have taken up more and more of
the organisers' time and we have had to decide to cut back to
just several weekend workshops a year or become emotionally
and physically 'played out'. We remain convinced that we can
only work constructively with the dying and bereaved, and with
their helpers in turn, by getting close to people emotionally
and to our own feelings in the process. That being so, it is
part and parcel of the job that at some time or other it all
becomes too much to bear; the helpers need maximum support from
those around them or, preferably, a complete break from such
work. It is part of our remit to relieve professional 'guilt'
about that but we have had to conquer our own before deciding
to tailor the number of workshops to our resources and not the
demand!

Are We Reaching Those Who Really Need It?
Despite this response, however, we are open to the charge that
we are only 'preaching to the converted' - and this on two
levels: the particular professional groups and the type of individuals within those groups who come to such workshops.

The groups who participate. We have been reassured by the variety of groups represented at the workshop (from those front-
line contacts one might have expected like social workers,
teachers and nurses, to those we would never have considered,
like the local government officers who have to hand out impersonal forms to the bereaved at a time of greatest distress and
feel extraordinarily 'cut-off' in the process) but it is true
that we have had great difficulty engaging two of the most
important - general practitioners and the clergy. It is the
author's experience that we are frequently invited to talk to

G.P. special interest groups on a variety of difficult
subjects, including bereavement, but that it is quite another
story to try and get G.P.s themselves to attend a workshop on
anything. That experience seems to be a general one; G.P.s
seem particularly resistant to exposing their own emotions to
such an extent. Levy and Balfour Sclare (1976) pointed out the
need for greater training in counselling techniques and have
been backed up by a demand for more courses at under/postgrad-
uate, medical-school level (Keane 1983). But nowhere is it
suggested that doctors, once in practice, need any further outlet to confront their own feelings. We can only hope that the
talking we do to G.P.s, and greater self-awareness built into
their original training, might gradually erode their professional defensiveness.

Perhaps we might have anticipated conflicting attitudes
from the clergy. On the one hand it must be difficult for those
who might be considered the natural 'experts' in the field to
admit to any need for personal help; on the other hand, we
might expect those who have had to struggle with painful insights during their professional training to be alive to the
continuing need for self-examination. The two ministers who
attended one of our workshops together illustrated the dilemma
perfectly. While one of them benefited enormously from the
experience and was able to extend greater empathy to the rest
of his group as a result, the second retreated into an archetypal religiose corner in which we were unable to reach him and
from which he launched such swingeing attacks on those who
could 'offer no hope' that we had to work hard both during and
after the workshop to repair damage he had done to social
workers already struggling with doubts about their
effectiveness.

We certainly do not agree that it is those with the firm-
est religious beliefs and the confirmed agnostics who are least
troubled by death anxieties because they have the greatest
sense of control and predictability (McMordie 1981). One of the
ministers attending proved brittly vulnerable; agnostics have
been shaken in their disbeliefs.

Some of the greatest contributions have been made by those
middle-of-the-road self-doubters whose beliefs are born of day-
to-day work in other professional fields where life and death
does not obey neat, pre-conceived philosophies and the practitioners are constantly challenged in their beliefs.

The individuals who participate. Even within those groups who
do come regularly to the workshops, it is always possible that
we get only those individuals who least need them - those who
are open and aware enough to attend a workshop in the first
place. Perhaps we might not be satisfying a hidden demand in
everyone, but creating just another vehicle for the emotional
groupie travelling from workshop to workshop in search of self-
enlightenment without ever quite reaching it!

Our experience over the years does not support such charges. Even if it were true that it were the least death-troubled who attend voluntary workshops (Telban 1981), we would consider it part of their strength that they recognise the need for continuing self-appraisal. Even if the workshops did attract the 'addicts', such attitudes are just one more form of defence, equivalent to the wallowers in grief amongst the dying and bereaved they might have to help, that we would feel appropriate to tackle in a workshop framework. In actual fact, the majority of those coming to the workshops have done so out of an uneasy awareness of their vulnerabilities, agonise over the decision to come, and work painfully but constructively through the feelings they knew would be aroused. The workshops accommodate people on widely different levels but ultimately with the same need. If that is more difficult to handle, it is also more rewarding.

## Arousal Of Feelings: Constructive Or Destructive

We have been accused too, of deliberately causing pain rather than fulfilling professional responsibilities to relieve it. We could point out, of course, that the workshops are voluntary and the people who attend have entered a contract the terms of which were fully laid before them in the advance publicity. We feel, however, that no matter how the ground is prepared, the impact of the experiential techniques we use is always a shock and if the only pretext for what we do was that people ought to know what they are letting themselves in for, it would be unethical indeed.

The charge is a serious one and analogous to the bitter complaints often made amidst the anger, guilt and misery of bereavement itself, that those trying to work with those emotions rather than suppress them, are making things worse not better. The answer can only be empirical. The majority of case-work in our lives as helpers with the bereaved is a product of grief repressed rather than grief experienced - no matter how painful the process in the short-run. And so also with the workshops - their value is proved in the long-term increase in self-awareness of those attending them and their greatly increased ability to help the dying and bereaved that is the ultimate aim (see below).

It was to achieve this, that the organisers found it necessary to make some alterations in the original format of the day to increase the opportunities to work at the feelings involved; in other words, we have resisted the temptation towards greater defences and have increased the experiential rather than the intellectual part of the programme.

## Coping With 'Casualties'

It is always difficult to assess where the necessary grief of the dying and bereaved slips over into 'pathology' - where defences become denial, healthy anger becomes generalised

hostility, 'normal' guilt becomes self-persecution, physical
reactions become psychosomatic 'illness', pre-occupation becomes withdrawal from the world. And so it is with the emotions
and behaviour of counsellors struggling with their own feelings
in a workshop experience designed to arouse and explore them
but not to leave the participants stuck in them without some
resolution.

'Casualties' are likely to result from a combination of
the process of group dynamics and the content of death under
discussion. The point at which 'rescue' is needed and how it
might be effected is a matter for the alertness, intuition and
expertise of the group leaders within the flexibility of the
day, but it is not only their responsibility. This is, after
all, a group experience and the group itself can and should be
used as a supportive medium. On occasions, it may even 'rescue'
one of its own facilitators - as when the author, at the end of
a particularly exhausting workshop, became increasingly concerned about the trauma of separation until one of the participants
suggested that perhaps we were dealing with the leader's
anxieties more than the group's!

Frequently, it will become obvious that a role-play, for
example, has so re-triggered the unresolved personal experience
of one of the participants that he or she needs extra attention
to prevent them from being hurt by the day. The day's plan may
be suspended temporarily to work with them on this by exploring
the experience in further role-play, sculpting and discussion.
While it would be wrong (both for the individual involved and
the rest of the group) to let one person become 'spotlighted',
it can also be very constructive for the group to see that
these feelings can be contained and worked through. The individual, in a sense, becomes a 'champion' of the group's feelings
and the author has seen the workshop experience helped immeas-
urably by the constructive exploration of something that would
have led to casualties if repressed or ignored. As with helping
the dying and bereaved themselves, we do more 'damage' by being
paralysed into not doing anything, than by opening things up.

More difficult to rescue, perhaps, are those individuals
who become unwittingly the sink for one of the more unpalatable
emotions aroused in all the participants - like anger or guilt
- which the group is only too 'pleased' to split off from themselves and project onto them. The task for the leaders is to
relieve the 'victim' by getting all the participants to own
their share of those feelings. It may be necessary to introduce
an exercise centred around that particular emotion itself and
what it means to every one of the participants.

Most difficult of all, in the author's experience, are
those individuals who become frozen by the experience and are
unable to let out any emotions at all for fear of what 'may
come out in the wash'. If the experiential nature of the workshop is made clear to would-be applicants and the workshop is
run with empathy, these should be rare instances but need

careful handling in order not to scar the individuals and the
watching group. The difficulty is not only how to cajole the
individual out of their corner but deciding when to abandon
this attempt and relieve the individual of the guilt (so often
felt by the bereaved surrounded by openly grieving others but
temporarily blocked in their own feelings) of not being able to
'join in'. In many cases, that relief in itself is enough to
allow them to come spontaneously out of the corner where greater efforts would have driven them further in; sometimes it is
better to back off!

Having said that, it is the author's experience that
casualties in general need to be 'chased' to some degree. We
have seen how that may be done within the session; follow-up of
casualties after the session is vital and in some cases will
reveal a need for deeper and more prolonged help and counselling for the counsellor themself and their family. One of the
most striking results of the workshops the author has run, has
been a number of self-referrals for therapy with their own
unresolved bereavements from participants. Work, for the workshop leaders, does not stop at the end of the workshop and it
would be highly irresponsible to go into the 'business' expecting it to!

Evaluation

What constitutes 'proper' evaluation, of course, is one of the
perennial problems of any social intervention technique. At
the moment, evaluation of our workshops is wholly subjective.
It relies on the personal reports of 'growth' in their own and
professional lives from those who have taken part that are very
much akin to the comments of nurses and other professionals
recorded in many studies (Laube 1977): 'I think about my own
feelings about death.....I allow myself to express my emotions
more freely.....share my experience with others in my work area
....I take time to really listen to a patient....listen to that
which is left unsaid.....communicate with family members'.

Clinically our initial impression is of an increased
referral rate of families for grief work by professionals more
keenly aware of client difficulties than their own increased
abilities to deal with them. Latterly, however, the demand has
been for top-up sessions and continuing support with cases they
retain in their care. There is less clinging to received expertise from workshop organisers and greater implementation of
their own skills and a call on support from their own professional hierarchies that we would see as appropriate but which
may come as a nasty surprise to those hierarchies themselves.
It is perhaps significant that we are getting increased applications to join workshops from senior members of social work,
health visitor and nursing administration and a scattering of
paediatric consultants!

Whether we should have a more 'scientific' approach to
evaluation is debatable. Many people have tried it but largely,

we feel, using criteria which are not particularly valid measures of what our workshops set out to do. We do not set out to lower death anxieties, merely acknowledge them as normal and healthy and, by providing an outlet for them, decrease the need to defend against them in ourselves and, therefore, those we are trying to help. In the last resort, evaluation based on 'scientific' measures like levels of death anxiety rely on subjective questionnaire answers in any case (Templer 1970).

The author feels that we should not decry the value of subjective report. We are dealing with the arousal and working through of subjective feelings and it is this awareness that is our aim. Nor, it would seem, is it particularly disturbing that what is learnt is sustained for variable periods (Yarber 1981). We would hope that the message to be gained from our workshops is not just that we need, as helpers, to be aware of our feelings about death and dying, but that we need to find continual means of sharing those feelings with our fellow professionals to prevent them interfering with the care of those we try to help.

THE FUTURE

Much of our future work, of course, will be in the ironing out of problems outlined above and in further refinement of our techniques; but there are other directions beckoning too.

Workshops For Target Groups

We have always resisted taking into each workshop a sizeable block from one professional group as they tend to form a sub-group in themselves, are stronger in their resistances together and tend to dominate the workshop with their particular needs. In this, our workshops are no different from the ordinary principles of group-work: blocks are blocks in all senses of the word. Nevertheless, we continue to receive mass applications from workers in particular professions or from their senior administrators on their behalf. As one possible way of dealing with this, the author has run an increasing number of workshops aimed at specific target groups on request and in their own premises and directed to their own particular needs.

There are many dangers in this. Operating alone, with repeated 'performances', one is apt to become a travelling roadshow bookable by widespread agencies with appropriate notice, peddling a slick star turn rather than true help. Every workshop needs to be just as carefully and individually thought out as the first; it needs to take account of the very particular needs of the particular branch of the particular professional group involved. A lot of the material is applicable across the board but people giving up a day or more to an intensive and painful experience need to know how they can apply what they have learnt to their particular work circumstances. They need just as much advance publicity and preparation and the opportunity afterwards to feed back what value or

otherwise they feel the workshops have been to them. The
itinerant workshop organiser needs close and continuing liaison
with the group he is aiming at if he is not to become a hit-and
-run merchant who at best achieves nothing and at worst leaves
behind him a trail of personal damage and professional disill-
usionment.

## Workshops For The Bereaved

As a further development, the author has begun to run workshops
for the bereaved themselves. Experiences with voluntary helping
agencies like Cruse, in which many of the workshop members were
recently bereaved, has convinced him that there would be value
in offering workshops to the bereaved as a group in addition to
the individual and family support they might already have
received. Not surprisingly, however, these workshops need very
careful planning. The defences against the emotions involved
are more easily than less easily punctured, bonds formed are
greater and the emotional discharge likely to be more intense.
He has found that they are best run on a two-day residential
basis which gives participants greater time and space to work
through their feelings with each other and the organiser alike.
Break-times become as important a chance to share feelings as
the programme itself and the author has spent exhausting nights
continuing conversations begun in earlier whole-group discussions. He has modelled the general structure of these workshops
much more closely on the stages of his grief-work with families,
with particular exercises devoted to joining, working-through
and separation. The whole weekend becomes a microcosm of grief-
work relationships and leaves the participants in a closer
supportive network of their own rather than mourning the loss
of the organiser as a new bereavement to be added to the one
with which they sought help.

## Follow-Up: Holding On Or Handing On

Finally, and appropriately so perhaps, there remains the question of follow-up. We have tended to see the issue of follow-up
in terms of the aftermath of our own particular workshops. We
have agonised over how best to keep contact with those who
attended our workshops and evaluate the personal impact on
them; how best to sustain the co-ordinated effort of different
professional groups that have found common ground in the intensity of the day. In truth, I think what we have really been
after is something more: to hold onto the close individual
relationships we inevitably form with those to whom we have
exposed such intimate feelings and the group warmth of shared
experience.

We cannot do so and nor would it be particularly appropriate. Just as those who work with the dying and bereaved have
to let go of their clients, so we as workshop organisers have
to let go of the helpers too. The future of death education
lies in the greater awareness of helpers with the dying and

bereaved, once aroused by our workshops, that they must find support within their own work circle.

We may bemoan a lack of 'quality control' (Crase 1980), but it should never become an excuse to hold onto the reins entirely ourselves. Death itself, the final emotional burial of the loved-one by the bereaved, the first letting-go by those who help with the bereaved, the end of a workshop for those helping the helpers: separation is, perhaps, the hardest lesson of all for us to learn. But only by facing up to it may emotional energy be made free to invest in new relationships elsewhere.

REFERENCES

Andrews, L. (1974) 'The Last Night', American Journal of
    Nursing, 74, 6 July, p. 1305
Annual Reports of the Health Service Commissioner (1980-81,
    1981-82, 1983-84), Her Majesty's Stationery Office
    Publications
Aries, P. (1981) The Hour of our Death, Allen Lane, London
Barton, D. et al (1975) 'The use of role-playing techniques as
    an instructional aid to teaching about death, dying and
    bereavement', Omega, 6, pp. 243-250
British Medical Journal (1974), Editorial, 'Talking about Death'
    British Medical Journal, 2, 20 April, pp. 131-132
British Medical Journal (1980), Editorial, 'Give Sorrow Words',
    British Medical Journal, 1 March, 280 (6214), p. 592
Crase, D.R. (1980) 'The Health Educator as Death Educator -
    Professional Preparation and Quality Control', Journal of
    School Health, 50, December, pp. 568-571
Crase, D.R. and Crase, D.C. (1974) 'Live Issues Surrounding
    Death Education', Journal of School Health, 44, February,
    pp. 70-73
Dickinson, G.E. (1981) 'Death Education in U.S. Medical Schools
    1975-80', Journal of Medical Education, 56(2), February,
    pp. 111-114
Duncome, D.C. (1974) 'Five Years at Yale: the Seminar on the
    Chronically Ill', Journal of Pastoral Care, 28, pp.152-163
Durlak, J.A. (1978) 'Comparison between experiential and
    didactic methods of death education', Omega, 9, pp. 57-66
Evans, B.J. (1982) 'The Death of a Classmate: a teacher's
    experience dealing with tragedy in the classroom', Journal
    of School Health, 52(2), February, pp. 104-107
Fredlund, D.J. (1977) 'Children and Death from the School
    Setting Viewpoint', Journal of School Health, 47(9),
    November, pp. 533-537
Freud, S. (1917) 'Mourning and Melancholia', in Collected
    Papers (1950) 4, pp. 152-172, Hogarth Press, London
Givelber, F. and Simon, B. (1981) 'A Death in the Life of a
    Therapist and its impact on the Therapy', Psychiatry, 44,
    May, pp. 141-149

Coping with Death: Helping the Dying and Bereaved

Hagglund, R.B. (1981) 'The Final Stage of the Dying Process',
  International Journal of Psychoanalysis, 62, Pt. 1.,
  pp. 45-49
Hammer, M. (1971) 'Reflections on one's own death as a peak
  experience', Mental Hygiene, 55, pp. 264-265
Hinton, J. (1980) 'Whom do dying patients tell?', British
  Medical Journal, 15 November, 281 (6251), pp. 1328-1330
Hinton, J. (1981) 'Sharing or withholding awareness of dying
  between husband and wife', Journal of Psychosomatic
  Research, 25(5), pp. 337-343
Hopping, B.L. (1977) 'Nursing students' attitude towards death',
  Nursing Research, 26(6), November-December, pp. 443-447
Keane, W.G. et al (1983) 'Death in Practice', Journal of the
  Royal College for General Practitioners, 33, June (251)
  pp. 347-351
Knight, M. and Field, D. (1981) 'A Silent Conspiracy: Coping
  with Dying Cancer Patients on an Acute Surgical Ward',
  Journal of Advanced Nursing, 6(3), May, pp. 221-229
Kubler-Ross, E. (1969) Death and Dying, Tavistock
  Publications, London
Laube, J. (1977) 'Death and Dying Workshop for Nurses: its
  effect on their Death Anxiety Level', International
  Journal for Nursing Studies, 14(3), pp. 111-120
Levy, B. and Balfour-Sclare, A. (1976) 'A Study of Bereavement
  in General Practice', Journal of the Royal College of
  General Practitioners, 26(166), May, pp. 329-336
Lewis, E. (1979) 'Mourning by the Family after a Stillbirth or
  Neonatal Death', Archives of Diseases in Childhood, 54,
  pp. 303-306
Maguire, P. (1975) 'The Psychological and Social Sequelae of
  Mastectomy', Ch. 9 in Perspectives in Psychological
  Aspects of Surgery
Marks, S.C. and Bertman, S.L. (1980) 'Experiences with learning
  about death and dying in the undergraduate anatomy
  curriculum', Journal of Medical Education, 55(1), January,
  pp. 48-52
McClam, T. (1980) 'Death Anxiety before and after Death
  Education: Negative Results', Psychological Report, 46(2),
  April, pp. 513-514
McMordie, W.R. (1981) 'Religiosity and Fear of Death: Strength
  of Belief System', Psychological Report, 49(3), December
  pp. 921-2
Murgatroyd, S. and Shooter, M. (1983) Unemployment, the Person
  and the Family, Unpublished
Nuttall, D. (1977) 'Attitudes to dying and the Bereaved',
  Nursing Times, 73(4), 13 October, pp. 1605-1607
Oakley, A., McPherson, A. and Roberts, H. (1984) Miscarriage,
  Fontana, London
Parkes, C.M. (1980) 'Bereavement Counselling: Does it Work?',
  British Medical Journal, 5 July, 281 (6232), pp. 3-6
Pincus, L. (1974) Death and the Family, Faber, London

Coping with Death: Helping the Dying and Bereaved

Porter, R. (1982) 'Essay Review: Death and the Doctors',
    Medical History, 26(3), July, pp. 335-341
Raphael, B. (1977)'Preventive intervention with the recently
    bereaved', Archives of General Psychiatry 34, pp.1450-1454
Saunders, C. (1972) 'A Therapeutic Community: St. Christopher's
    Hospice', in Psychological Aspects of Terminal Care,
    Schoenberg, B., Catt, A., Perekz, D. and Kurscher, A. (eds)
    Columbia University Press, New York
Silver, R.T. (1980) 'The Dying Patient: A Clinician's View',
    American Journal of Medicine, 68(4), April, pp. 473-475
Sonstegard, L. (1976) 'Dealing with Dying: The Grieving Nurse'
    American Journal of Nursing, 76(9), 2 September,
    pp. 1490-1492
Stedeford, A. (1981) 'Couples Facing Death II - Unsatisfactory
    Communication', British Medical Journal (Clinical Research)
    24 October, 283 (6299), pp. 1098-1101
Stedeford, A. (1979) 'Psychotherapy of the Dying Patient',
    British Journal of Psychiatry', 135, July, pp. 7-14
Telban, S.G. (1981) 'Death Anxiety and Knowledge about Death',
    Psychology Report, 49(2), October, p. 648
Templer, D.I. (1970) 'The Construction and Validating of a
    Death Anxiety Scale', Journal of General Psychology, 82,
    pp. 165-177
Vaisrub, S. (1974) Editorial: 'Dying is Being Worked to Death',
    Journal of the American Medical Association, 229,
    30 September, pp. 1909-1910
Weisman, A.D. (1981) 'Understanding the Cancer Patient: the
    Syndrome of the Care-Giver's Plight', Psychiatry, 44, May
    pp. 161-168
Yarber, W.L. et al (1981) 'Effect of Death Education on
    Nursing Students' Anxiety and Locus Control', Journal of
    School Health, May, pp. 367-372

Chapter Seven

WORKING WITH SEXUALITY

Dick Pates

INTRODUCTION

Sex is one of the strongest of human drives, something that is
universal and natural and not a subject usually taught in a
formal way. We arrive at our own sexuality through different
sorts of learning, conditioning and experience, so should workshops on the subject be necessary? Sex, despite its universality
and inevitability, despite its essential role in procreation,
is still the subject of embarrassment and ignorance, especially
with regard to others. The emphasis of this chapter, therefore,
is on communication with others regarding sex and sexuality.
    The content of the chapter is the result of the experience
of having run a number of workshops over a three-year period.
These have been for different groups, for differing durations,
with the discoveries of one workshop being put into the next so
that a model has been developed. This is essentially a personal
view, gleaned from experience and as a part of a process that
is ongoing. The important feature of the workshops is that they
are experiential and that they are never seen to be lectures or
for the purpose of providing hard facts, but are a way of looking
at sexuality, the issues raised and attitudes and ideas arising.

Why Workshops?
The decision to run workshops as a learning experience is based
on two complementary reasons. Firstly, from a personal point of
view it is felt to be more comfortable using this method of
learning; the degree of personal involvement needed removes the
distancing effect that didactic teaching can achieve. It is
felt that because of the emotional nature of the subject, a
closer, interpersonal style of working is needed. Secondly,
this is borne out by others' experience of teaching sexuality
matters. Dow and Sclare (1982) found that medical undergraduates
showed a preference for a small group discussion to supplement
lectures and multi-disciplinary panel discussions for learning
about psychosexual problems. Bell et al (1979) found that when
training clinical psychologists the use of role-play and other

group activities were important aspects of training in human sexuality.

## Should Sexuality Be Taught?
The question of whether sexuality should be a subject that is taught or not has attracted controversy in the past and to some extent still does. This is especially true when dealing with the aspects of sex education in schools - should it be taught or left to parents? The question of responsibility and the passage of personal values is highly relevant here and has been hotly debated elsewhere, e.g. Steinbacher (1984) and Parrott (1984) provide an interesting discussion about the merits and demerits of this question especially from a religious perspective. Philliber and Tatum (1982) discovered that a sex education course which increased sexual knowledge neither encouraged nor discouraged the sexual activity amongst the subjects involved or that it removed the role of instruction from the home. In the area of mental handicap, one still comes across the parental and professional views that suggest that knowledge leads to action and therefore is undesirable, the assumption being that lack of knowledge leaves these persons safe in ignorance   (Craft and Craft 1981, 1982). This controversy cannot be dealt with in an unbiased way in this chapter for the very nature of the chapter and book presupposes the workshop method is worthwhile and that the subject of human sexuality is one subject amenable to this type of experience. However, it is also true that when requests are made for workshops, the groups or individuals making that request feel that a need exists and therefore that the request is meeting a demand. It would be inappropriate to use this format when participants objected to the subject matter and it would, of course, not be functionally feasible to run such a workshop without willing participation. It is also important to be able to run the workshops on one's own terms; the offer of running the workshop should clearly include responsibility for style and content being with the person running the workshop. This should be explicitly negotiated at the first contact so that both parties are clear about the contract.

## What Should These Workshops Include?
The aims of running workshops on sexuality will be expanded later. This chapter explores the reasons for doing this work and the anticipated changes that this will produce for the participants. One question that needs to be raised early is, can the content realise the aims of the workshop? Dow and Sclare (op.cit.) maintain that the three principal, interdependent areas that are essential to any training in sexuality are attitudes, skills and information. Attitudes and skills are dealt with in terms of the nature of the workshop and the exercises subsequently described, but the question of information impinges upon the area of sex education for sexual

knowledge. This was not initially seen to be the role of a
workshop on sexuality because sex education is a large area in
itself, but the educative part of this subject cannot be
separated from the passage of factual information, especially
where myths need to be explored and beliefs examined.

On questioning people from sixteen to sixty in workshops,
concerning the level of sex education that they had had and
from where it came, a wide diversity of answers have been
received. Typically, however, it is evident that much of the
responsibility for the acquisition of sexual knowledge has been
outside the home, or inadequately dealt with within the home
and the teaching in schools has often been woefully lacking.
This situation is changing but it is still apparent that there
are wide differences in levels of sexual knowledge attained by
the school leaver and the methods of that transmission of
knowledge.

## Is Sex Education Not Sufficient?

It can be argued that were sex education adequately accom-
plished in early life, then the training of people subsequently
would be unnecessary, but it is inevitable that information
gained at adolescence will be inadequate for later needs if
one's role in life is involved with other people's sexuality.
The amount of the knowledge that can be acquired early in life
may be adequate for coping with adolescence and early adult
sexuality from a 'user's view point, but when dealing later
with, for example, cancer sufferers, spinally injured patients,
the mentally handicapped etc., more specialised knowledge may
be required as well as being able to cope with possible
attitude changes. It is important, therefore, to include an
educative component where this is necessary, but this is not
usually the prime aim of the workshop.

## Why Are Workshops Requested?

Reasons for being asked to run a workshop on sexuality are many
and diffuse, as are the ages, experiences and roles of the
intended participants. There are aspects of running workshops
on sexuality that will have much in common with workshops on
other subjects but there are also other aspects that differ
fundamentally. For these reasons, it is not possible to provide
a 'blueprint' for running workshops on sexuality.

It is important to remember that we are all sexual beings,
whether or not we are in relationships, whether or not we have
or have had sexual experiences and whether or not we have the
full physical and mental abilities to sustain or understand
sexual feelings and responses. We may be equipped to understand
sex, but may need help in doing so. Sexuality, therefore, it
can be argued should be a part of a person's range of experience as much as any other experience may be and as such
parallels other areas of skills training on one hand and
counselling training on the other.

## What Level Of Knowledge Can Be Assumed?

Despite the fact of sexuality being universal and inevitable,
it is also cloaked with embarrassment, ignorance and mythology
and the possible extent of this should be realised before
attempting to run a workshop. Having once been told during a
workshop that a nun teaching in a convent sanctioned oral sex
in 'proper relationships' because she assumed that this referred to kissing, having argued with bewildered peers at age
twelve about the function of a sheath and having realised
whilst working with sixteen year olds that some parents still
totally deny the sexuality of their offspring, it becomes
apparent that little can be assumed about the status quo of
sexual attitudes and knowedge prior to a workshop. One of the
roles of the workshop will be to explode the myths and reduce
and cope with the embarrassment, but the existence of these,
needs to be acknowledged at the outset. Running a workshop on
sexuality can be seen to be a voyeuristic experience by out-
siders and by participants before the start and your participants may have difficulty in being with you from the beginning.
This should not be underestimated and participants may
anticipate that their sexuality will be exposed to their
colleagues during the workshop. Ways of coping with this will
be explored later but it is important to realise that this is
one of the basic and fundamental issues which will be around
at the very start of the workshop.

## The Need For Caution And Sensitivity

While taking a facilitative or exploratory role (which some
will see as provocative) in organising these workshops it is
necessary to be responsive to the needs and feelings of others
regarding sexuality. You, as organiser, facilitator, have your
own views which may or may not be acceptable to others, as have
your participants, and it needs to be made clear at the
beginning that attitudes and personal codes of morality of
yourself and participants are neither right nor wrong and that
whatever your position you can always find someone else with
a more extreme view than yourself or who would totally disagree
with you. Dow and Sclare (op.cit.) maintain 'one can scarcely
under estimate the importance of personal values and attitudes
in our acceptance, assessment and management of sexually
related issues. No man or woman however naive, approaches sexual issues neutrally, each brings to the subject his or her own
experiences, responses and values'. Differences should be the
basis for discussion rather than criticism. Before stating that
which you perceive as being objective fact regarding sexuality,
remember that your sexuality is going to be a strong influence
on the workshop and therefore needs to be thought about
carefully whenever controversy arises or you are making a point.
It is difficult to be honestly objective about sexuality
without impinging your own sexual subjectivity upon it.

The concepts that participants will have about what will

be happening in the workshop will vary greatly. They may be imagined as being wild, exposing and controversial, asking one to do things that are totally out of character (e.g. Albery 1984) or may be perceived as a fairly passive passage of information or knowledge such as in a study day (e.g. Sebba 1981). It is important when organising a workshop to make it clear to the parties requesting the workshop that they will involve people sharing thoughts and feelings but that they will not be asked to do bizarre things which are outside their realm of experience. A fear of the unknown may be useful to a degree to heighten the state of attention of the participants but one should also be sensitive to the vulnerability of others. A valuable motto for these workshops could be: 'Don't do unto others what you would not have done unto yourself'.

THE AIMS OF THE WORKSHOPS

The aims of the workshops vary slightly according to the group of people with whom you are dealing, but basically are three:

To increase the awareness of participants' own sexuality. It is extremely hard to talk to others in an honest and helpful way if feelings about one's own sexuality are confused or repressed. By use of large group, small group and dyadic discussion, role-play etc., it is hoped that barriers can be lowered and an honest perception of one's own sexuality can be established. This may seem unnecessary, but experience has shown that people are often unwilling to acknowledge their own sexuality in relation to others.

To increase the awareness of others' sexuality. As hard as it may be for people to talk about their own sexuality, it is often as hard to talk about or to acknowledge the sexuality of others. This is particularly so if the other party happens to be disadvantaged by mental or physical infirmity or by age. To accept that the mentally handicapped, the physically handi-capped, the chronically sick, the young, the old and even one's own parents are all sexual beings and are capable of feelings and responses is not something that has always been generally held to be so in the past and even today is not a universally held belief. The 'swinging 60's' and the 'permissive 70's' were, if we are to believe many contemporary sources, the sexual liberation of the young, trendy and healthy but not the rest of society. Even for non-disadvantaged groups the accep-tance of their sexuality is not automatic.

To be able to discuss sexuality with others. This is relevant when a workshop is being run for the benefit of a particular group. This may not seem essentially different from the previous aim, but while it is one thing to accept the sexuality of others, it is quite another to be able and willing to talk

140

to them about it. It may seem that this view is orientated towards groups with specified difficulties, but it is hard to imagine any group of people to whom this does not apply, whether they are a group labelled by their particular handicap or a couple experiencing difficulties in a relationship or a friend who needs to work through some personal problems.

The aims may seem loose and arbitrary, but I believe them to be the foundations of successful work in this field and without which it is difficult to imagine the ability to function in dealing with others' sexuality.

## Different Needs Of Different Groups

When a request is received to run a workshop on sexuality, then it is usual for the person making the request to have some particular aim in mind. It may be for a group of people who potentially will benefit from the workshop, a group who feel the need for education in the area, an identifiable client group for whom advice is needed or a group for whom knowledge is available but where counselling techniques are needed. Whatever the group and whatever the eventual aim of the workshop, many of the aspects of organisation and content will be common to workshops for all these groups.

There is sometimes an assumption that those in our care represent only the diagnosis with which they have been labelled and that the corollaries of these are mainly practical issues. With more thought it becomes clear that the area of sexuality is relevant to many conditions. Attwell (1984) describes how rarely cancer sufferers are counselled about sexuality even though patients may have had disfiguring operations such as breast removal or operations such as colostomies that will produce body changes and patterns of behaviour, may have impotence as a result of treatment or have great emotional difficulties due to the impact of illness. Yet, according to Attwell, many health professionals do not discuss sexuality or sexual functioning with their patients because of personal value conflicts or because of feelings of inadequacy about this subject.

Zwerner (1982) reported a study on the provision of sexuality counselling services for women who had suffered spinal cord injury which showed that less than half of the subjects questioned had received any counselling post injury, but 85% had felt that some individual or group counselling would have been useful for their sexual adjustment. Kitzinger (1982) emphasises the need for sexuality counselling during pregnancy and in a post partum period. Often during this period of a woman's life there are fears about damage to the unborn baby or religious taboos about sexual activity, but that this is a time of great importance for the couple and the changes that occur as a result of pregnancy and childbirth should be recognised.

In addition to the three above mentioned references, other groups may be in need of counselling or education, e.g. those suffering from heart problems, the mentally handicapped, the physically handicapped, adolescents in care, the elderly etc. and frequently the person who is asked about a problem or for advice is not necessarily the person in charge. It is more likely to be the person with whom the individual has most contact and with whom a trust has been established. It is, therefore, important to recognise the needs of others in your care or trust who might approach you with a problem or a worry and the need to be able to cope with that request and not merely be embarrassed or pass the responsibility to another individual.

The differential needs for different groups should be addressed in the planning stage of the workshop. One aspect of planning that is frequently underestimated by those requesting workshops is the time needed to cover a realistic programme, so that when relating sexuality to a particular topic or group, it is necessary to spend part of the workshop on general matters of sexuality and warming-up the group and use the latter part of the workshop for the more specific work. By this stage, the participants may realise they need more time (half a day or one day is rarely sufficient to reach a stage of feeling that enough has been achieved). Invariably follow-up sessions are requested.

The following are examples of workshops run for specific client groups:

Training workshops as a pre-requisite for running sex education courses for the mentally handicapped. Having covered in the early part of the workshop the issues of individual sexuality and the warming-up process of the group, one then looks at matters of how the mentally handicapped acquired their knowledge of sexuality and the differences they have compared to other members of society who may have wider access to sexual knowledge. Other components of the day's workshop would be looking at attitudes regarding the sexuality of the mentally handicapped and the prejudices that exist with this client group and explore some of the myths that are likely still to be extant in the community. Other sessions will cover the sort of materials that one would use in a sex education course for the mentally handicapped. These need to be very carefully selected because it may be that the people one is trying to train have an insufficient grasp of abstract thinking which would render many diagrammatic illustrations incomprehensible. It is, therefore, necessary that both the materials and the teaching methods for this group of clients need to be looked at very carefully in a workshop. Another issue that is particularly relevant to this client group are the legal and moral issues related to the caring of a group who are sometimes deemed by law not to be capable of making their own decisions. Role-play will be used in the workshop as well, to try to enact some situations where specific help is required either as a result of complaints or

problems of confrontation and this becomes a very valuable
tool with staff working with mentally handicapped people.

Workshop for awareness training - staff working with
rehabilitation patients. The staff working with patients who
are recovering from potentially crippling conditions, e.g.
spinal injury, coronary disease, chronic respiratory problems
etc., often require advice and counselling regarding future
capabilities, handicaps and difficulties and it has been
noticed that the patients will approach staff with whom they
are working closely and whom they can trust. This may not be
an identified person who has training or knowledge regarding
sexuality and prognosis of the future sexuality activity. It
is necessary to enable the staff to cope with the situations
in which they find themselves. Again the first aim of the
workshop will be fulfilled in the early sessions, the second
and third aim will need to be approached so that the participants feel that they can cope when requests are made of them.
The feelings of inadequacy they may have at dealing with problems is explored as is the counselling function and sexual
knowledge related to this client group; even if they are not
able to respond clinically to questions this means they can
provide some sort of guidance to the appropriate source for
the patient.

In this workshop the existing knowledge of the participants is examined with regard to what they understand about
certain conditions and the difficulties that people might have
of coping after, for example, spinal injury and the alternatives are explored for sexual fulfilment. One important aspect
is being able to pinpoint alternatives for people who previously have regarded sexual intercourse as being the only means
of sexual fulfilment. Role-play is again used with this
workshop and is a very useful way of exploring the difficult
issues of being approached about sexual matters or having to
go to other people for advice about the handling of these
matters. For example, how a nurse or physiotherapist might
handle the first shy questionings about sexual functioning
following an accident or how to handle an incident of sexual
harassment on a ward where perhaps there is a high level of
unexpended sexual energy! In addition, an area which needs to
be explored where the participants may be staff involved in
close bodily contact, such as physiotherapists or occupational
therapists, part of the workshop is used to examine the difficulty of performing what to the rest of us is a very intimate
function, i.e. having physical contact with a stranger and a
breaking down of the taboos that this involves. Although it is
part and parcel of the work for these therapists, for the
recipient it may be a very stimulating experience in a clinical
environment and the perception of the recipient needs to be
examined.

<u>Workshops with people working with adolescents, or with adolescents themselves</u>. With this group the initial parts of the workshop are still common in looking at an individual's sexuality and the 'warming-up' process. However, this part of the work is carried out in a more substantial way because it is often at this level that there is greater need.

An emphasis here might need to be on social skills type training for helping socially unskilled individuals initiate relationships, providing specific information about factual matters such as contraception, providing an arena for discussion of contemporary morality and social mores (this may be more necessary than with other groups), reflecting a need not to overestimate your group's understanding and level of knowledge. Street wise kids can still carry a lot of ignorance around with them!

With this group of people it is also very important not to use one's own experience as a way of showing distance and, therefore, belittling the potential lack of experience of the participants who may be feeling that they are a little at sea in an adult world. It is also interesting to note how attitudes do change and one needs to keep abreast of the changes that occur and explore with the group what their kind of thinking is and what the attitudes of their peers are regarding sexuality and other interpersonal issues. For example, I have found that girls' attitudes to the importance of virginity are different when the views of present day sixteen to eighteen year olds are compared to those who were in late adolescence twenty to thirty years ago. This type of group may have greater inhibitions at the outset, but once those initial fears are calmed, provide a very stimulating group.

These three brief illustrations show the need to think about the client group and integrate parts of a programme which may need to be specifically designed for this group. It may also be important to vary the depth and pace of the workshop with respect to the experience and background of the participants. If groups of individuals are well acquainted with each other and are vastly experienced in their client group, they may take to things more quickly and easily than a group who are generally strangers and new to their chosen field of work.

PRACTICAL ASPECTS OF THE WORKSHOP

The success of the workshop will depend partly on careful planning, but not only is the programme an important factor but the practical aspects of organisation that are carried out beforehand are also crucial.

<u>Space And Materials</u>
Because of the potentially threatening nature of the subject efforts·should be made to ensure that the participants' room is

as comfortable as possible and all necessary services provided.
Rooms should be adequately heated, of a sufficient size to
allow for breaking up into small groups, or with the provision
of extra rooms for this purpose, carpeted if possible, as at
some stage the participants may be required to sit or lie on
the floor and free from the distraction of other activities in
the vicinity. Rooms should also be private and not overlooked
by other people.
      Materials need to be provided such as large flip charts,
felt pens, overhead projectors, pencils, papers and feedback
material. These may seem obvious, but their omission does
provide a source of some difficulty!

## Meal Breaks

Provision of tea and coffee for morning breaks (and the
facility for people to smoke during these breaks if they so
wish) is important so that the participants do not have to
break up and go elsewhere for refreshment. If the workshop is
a whole day, then lunch should be provided and brought to the
site, or participants could be asked to bring lunch with them
or asked to provide some food for a communal lunch. It is
important to have lunch provided on site by whichever means
so that your group stays together through lunch and maintains
the cohesion that has been established during the morning and
is not distracted by other matters such as shopping or work at
lunchtime! This may seem trivial, but means that re-starting
the afternoon session is easier if the cohesion of the morning
is still present.

## Duration

It will probably be found that it is not worthwhile to run a
workshop on the basis of less than one day's duration, for it
takes some time at the beginning to get the group relaxed and
into the subject and a three-hour period is not really long
enough to cover an adequate amount of material. If a half-day
session is in the afternoon, people come from work thinking of
work and if it is in the morning, they will have appointments
to go to and they will lose concentration by the end of the
session. A full day is probably the minimum time necessary for
a successful workshop. Participants should be asked to keep
the whole day free and not expect to work after the workshop.

## Group Size

Having decided on the practical aspects of space and equipment,
the number in the group needs to be determined and the programme
provided. It is important that the group is of a size that is
comfortable both from the organisers' point of view and the
participants, a group of ten to twelve is probably the optimum
number, a number that is large enough to break into small
groups and dyads which can be reformed into new groupings
several times and small enough for participants to feel

identifiable as a group and for a cohesion to be established. It is also difficult with larger groups to remember names of people just introduced and to ensure that all participants are heard and seen not just pushed into the background by more forceful members. An upper limit of sixteen group members has been found to work, but this is probably more difficult than a smaller group.

## Programme
The programme should be clearly defined well before the day so that the day hangs together coherently and that there is adequate spare material if any part of the day falls flat or if it finishes before its allotted time. In practice this rarely happens, but one needs to be sure that material is available. This also means that the day should be sufficiently flexible to allow for developments that occur during the sessions. To this end it may be advantageous not to issue a programme in advance other than to discuss with the agency requesting the workshop what the general topics will be. It is not realistic to have dictated to a workshop organiser what the content will be, for it is the organiser who is providing the expertise. By having the programme clearly in mind and also only broadly outlined in the minds of the participants, it will give flex- ibility and will not create too much anxiety for the particip- ants before the day of the workshop. Even the choice of title is important, to be sufficiently flexible and non-threatening and acceptable to those funding the day! It should also reflect the relationship and emotional aspect of sexuality and not just the physical aspects of this subject.

## THE WORKSHOP

The following is a plan or schedule for the workshop based on several that have taken place, it follows a general outline and would be adapted as necessary to particular client groups. In planning the workshop cognisance will need to be taken of the needs of the group for whom the workshop is intended. Although the workshop follows a general model, inevitably individual and group needs should be recognised. It is not intended to be a sexual instruction course or to be a training course for those involved in sex therapy. Intended participants are those whose daily work involves contact with others when sexuality may be an issue or in the case, for example, of adolescents, of a self awareness process. The format has proved successful insofar as the feedback received after the workshop has indicated that the purposes of the workshop have been achieved.

The day starts with an introduction by the leaders, of themselves, explaining who they are, what they do and their interest in the subject of sexuality. The length of time taken with introductions should be of sufficient length to allow participants to settle and feel at home in their surroundings.

This is an important stage to be achieved in a comfortable
manner, for at this point the leaders will probably feel a
degree of anxiety, thinking about the way the day will unfold
and the possible pitfalls that may occur during the day. The
participants will also feel anxious because of the uncertainty
about what the day will produce and the sharing of intimacy
with strangers. Although the purpose of the day will be to
explore, confront and provoke discussions and for this a degree
of psychological arousal will probably be beneficial, it is
necessary to reassure the participants who feel most threatened
at this point about the non-threatening nature of the leaders!
Because of the difficult nature of the subject, participants
are also told at this stage that they may have access to the
leaders after the workshop, in the event of the need to discuss
items or difficulties that have arisen from the workshop. This
is done via a work telephone number.

Following the introduction of themselves, one of the
leaders will talk briefly about the need for the interchange
of the day to be kept confidential within the group. It is
hoped that what will be learnt will be of use to the participants, but given the honesty that people are being asked to offer,
the corollary is that this degree of mutual confidentiality
should be maintained after the group has dispersed. Participants are also told that they will be encouraged to discuss,
argue and challenge anyone, including the leaders but their
respect for others' views is requested. Given the wide backgrounds and experience of participants, this needs to be re-
inforced. Leaders especially need to be non-judgemental.

The participants are then asked to introduce themselves
and to say a little about themselves as a way of introduction.
This is done with one proviso - that everyone present will use
forenames during this day and that any individual rank will be
disregarded for the day. This is important where one might be
training a group of staff where some of the staff supervise
or are employees of the others. This is the one strict rule
that is laid down by the leader to ensure that rank does not
inhibit the processes of the day. The introductions are done
by each person introducing the person next to her and then
herself in a cumulative fashion so that the last person has to
introduce the whole group, having had most names already
rehearsed. This is a useful exercise for remembering names but
also to introduce a level of humour where some recall of names
becomes difficult and thus acts as another ice breaker.

By this stage (which has taken about ten to fifteen
minutes) the participants still have little idea of what the
day will be and how threatening it will be other than the
title of the day and statements about confidentiality. The
participants are asked to divide into couples and discuss with
each other their anxieties and expectations about the day. They
are asked to state what they think will be covered in the day,
what they would like to have covered and what they are worried

about. The couples are then asked to report back to the group about the thoughts expressed by their partners. This exercise serves several important purposes. First, it introduces the informal, discursive style of the day and makes people participate immediately. Secondly, it allows people to express their fears and vulnerabilities openly so that these can be acknowledged. Thirdly, it allows them to see that their fears, far from being idiosyncratic are shared by the majority of the group and therefore illustrate a fairly natural anxiety. Fourthly, it provides feedback for the leaders about the state of thinking and anxiety of the participants. And finally, gives an indication as to what the participants are expecting in terms of content.

The concerns that are usually expressed are about the need for self disclosure of sexual activity or opinions and the content is usually anticipated as being an acquisition of greater knowledge regarding sexuality. The leaders can then use this material to respond to the participants' expectations and to voice their own expectations and anxieties about the day. The emphasis of the response is that no individual will be put in a position of self disclosure unless that is comfortable, no-one will be coerced into doing anything they do not wish to do and that the day is essentially participative rather than a series of lectures on sexuality. The content is explained as being a series of exercises examining various areas of sexuality where attitudes and ideas are as important as knowledge and that the amount of knowledge obtained from the day may be limited, but that it is more important to be able to use the knowledge acquired than just knowing facts.

The leaders also respond with their expectations, these might be:
1. That participants will enjoy the day.
2. That they will feel more confident in talking about sexuality.
3. That they will question the leaders and each other now and after the workshop.
4. That they may feel confident about tackling the problems that arise.

Before proceeding to the next stage of the workshop one of the leaders issue what has come to be called a 'vulnerability caveat'. This is a statement from one of the leaders reminding all the participants that we are all sexual beings, that it is a potentially difficult subject for all and we need to explore ourselves before teaching others. The continuum of sexual liberality is explained i.e. that viewpoints regarding sexuality are not bi-polar but a continuum; where a person places themselves on that continuum is a personal decision. Inevitably some will be more conservative or more liberal than others about some issues, personal values should not be pushed as being correct; listen and respect.

The next exercise involves a change in pace and is crucial to the aims of the workshop in lowering inhibitions and talking about sex. This is an exercise on the language of sex. It is one that causes much embarrassment and difficulties in starting but once achieved, makes the rest of the day an easier experience. Sex is talked of in language that reflects an impersonal and clinical feeling about sexuality, that achieves distance and therefore feels safe by disassociation. We can talk more easily about sexual intercourse or genitalia than we can use common language and by doing so talk at a different level than we would if talking to spouse, lovers or other intimates. If, as an individual you are approached by another with a request for help on a matter of sexuality, or if that need is perceived, it may be inappropriate to talk in a different code of language to that person. Therefore, it is important to be able to use the same language as the person with whom one is working, although,of course, it is not an issue that should be forced unnaturally.

The main aims of the exercise are as stated, to lower inhibitions about discussing sex and using vernacular language tends to do this quickly and also to introduce the idea of the need to understand other people's phraseology about sexuality.

It is explained to participants that common language of sex is used naturally and we wish to discover what vernacular words are used. Each participant is given a piece of paper and asked to divide it into six columns. At the top of the columns are written the words: Sexual Intercourse, Male Genitalia, Female Genitalia, Menstruation, Orgasm and Masturbation. They are then given ten minutes to write down as many words as they can think of that describe the words at the top of the columns. The leader will then put the column headings onto a blackboard or an overhead projector and ask the participants to call out suitable words. The initial response is usually silence so the leader needs to contribute the first one on each column. Once the ice is broken, then words tend to be produced quickly. Experience has shown that twenty-five words will be produced for sexual intercourse and slightly fewer for the other columns. What is interesting is that on each occasion, some new words (at least new to the leaders) emerge and feedback on this is valuable! This is one exercise that breaks down inhibitions quickly and the rest of the day proceeds with a greater degree of relaxation.

The next exercise consists of an examination of viewpoints on sexuality. This is prefaced by a discussion about how we acquire a knowledge of sexuality and how potentially biasing the effects of jokes, stories, books, films, T.V., siblings, friends, pornography etc., can be in describing sexuality to someone with little knowledge or experience. Too often it appears that sexuality is portrayed in an unrealistic and often sexist light and without any emotional relevance. Two passages are read to the participants; the passages remain unidentified

at the beginning and at the end of each passage participants
are asked to write down their first thoughts about the passages,
the relevance of this to their own experience and they are
asked to guess whether the authors are male or female. The
passages can be selected from many different sources that
illustrate some area of explicit sexuality. Two that have been
used successfully are 'The French Lieutenant's Woman', pages
303-304, (Fowles 1969), the section describing the seduction
of Sarah Woodruff, and a section of a short story by Anais Nin,
'The Veiled Woman', from the Delta of Venus, pages 88-90 (Nin
1977), which describes the erotic seduction of a man by a
mysterious woman. The use of these extracts illustrates a
diverse portrayal of sexuality, the differences in perspective
when seen from a male or female point of view and the statements of sexuality stripped of romanticism. The styles of
writing are oddly balanced in that the majority of participants
identify the first extract as being written by a woman and the
second by a man whereas the reverse is true. This is a useful
point to make about expectations of sexuality.

The discussion that follows this can be led according to
the comments produced but will make people think about sexuality and the facilitating commentary can be used regarding
whether the portrayal is realistic and whether this builds up
false views on sexuality. The fact that fiction often ignores
the practical aspects of sex can be introduced here.

By the end of this first session and a welcome coffee
break, we have covered initial thoughts, broken down some
taboos on language, discovered viewpoints on sexuality and had
people talking freely about sexuality.

The second session is conducted by splitting the group
into small groups. A workshop leader will be involved with
each group to participate and facilitate the group if necessary.
The group is provided with a number of stimulus statements,
(the number being twice the number of participants per sub-
group), which are used to stimulate discussion. The statements
(see Appendix for fuller list) are stated opinions of various
subjects pertaining to sexuality and are typed on slips of
paper. The statements are so written as to provoke discussion,
e.g. 'It's not surprising so many women are raped, the way
they dress they are asking for it'; 'The age of consent for
sex should be abandoned'; 'Most people find pornography a turn-
on'. The members of the group are asked to take turns in picking up one of the statements from the floor, reading the
statement to the group, making a statement about what their
reaction to the statement is and then chairing a discussion
with the other members of the group. It is important to
encourage participants to be truthful in their statements and
for the group leader not to hide behind 'the devil's advocate'
position.

This exercise tends to generate a lot of energy and
discussion and heighten the ability of the group to discuss

matters of sexuality. In each of the groups it is emphasised
that group members do not have to give their own opinion
necessarily, but should address the subject at some level.
Experience has shown that people tend to react quickly and
honestly and the main difficulty is keeping order in the group
if an item proves controversial so that everyone has a chance
of speaking. This exercise usually takes the workshop to the
lunch break, but before breaking for lunch the whole group is
brought together briefly to check that no-one has burning
issues or worries that need to be addressed before the break.

After the lunch break, before starting on the afternoon
session, an energiser game is used to reactivate participants,
after their lunch. This is a game requiring energetic activity
for about ten minutes.

The afternoon is divided into two sessions, the first
being a role-play session and the second a whole group discussion. The content of the role-play session will vary greatly
with the type of group at the workshop. If, for example, the
group is a single profession group, then at this stage the
work will be orientated towards their field of work.

When working with people who work with the mentally
handicapped, scenes are devised which are typical of
confrontation situations and participants are required to role-
play these in groups of three or four people. Different roles
are given to people via descriptions of the roles being played
and their perception of the situation. Each individual is given
a slightly different script which replicates the sort of position found in this area. Situations such as discussions about
the rights of individuals to masturbate or inappropriate handling of sexual parts by others are the sort of scenes that are
role-played.

With adolescents, the role-play would be more appropriately linked with assertiveness training and courting ritual.
By using cross gender roles here it can help to facilitate
understanding of the other's gender role in these sort of
situations. For example, a girl would be asked to try to ask a
boy out which may be much against their cultural norms. The
role-playing of telling parents about a teenage pregnancy or
requesting advice at a Family Planning Clinic are also typical.

With other professional groups the role-plays would be
devised to cover areas mentioned before the workshop as being
of relevance. These are usually situations that are understood
to be difficult and often follow a counselling mode for discussion of sexual problems. Usually only one or two scenes can
be role-played in the time and are done in groups of three or
four with all group members involved or with observers feeding
back information to the group.

With all the role-plays great care is needed to establish
the scene properly before the start. Ensure that people are in
role and take it seriously. This is only achieved by explaining
the point of the exercise before the start and the necessity

for approaching it seriously. A discussion about the problem with the group whilst still in role is also needed to understand the impact of the role and feelings it generated plus adequate debriefing at the end to ensure that participants are out of role.

For the final session, which will be the last hour of the day, all the participants and leaders come together in a group to discuss anything that has come up in the day in a large forum, argue controversial matters, discuss what relevance this has to their professional groups, what is needed in the future and what has been inadequate about the day. At the end the participants are asked to complete a feedback form and the group is closed promptly at the end of the allotted time.

This is a description of a one-day workshop. If this were continued over two days, then the afternoon sessions would be greatly expanded to include more relevant work for that profession, especially in the area of role-play and discussion of professional matters to do with sexuality in a group format.

Variations can be made to this format with the use of different exercises, or the inclusion of other aspects. But the general format tends to be used as an outline for any group.

OTHER ISSUES RELATED TO THE WORKSHOP

Leadership

Experience has shown that it is preferable for the workshop to be led by two people rather than one. It has been found that when running workshops with one leader it imposes a lot of stress on that leader who has to be aware of all of the dynamics of the group and also to cover all the aspects throughout the day. However, it is difficult to share the leadership of the group with another person unless that person is sufficiently familiar with one's style of working. Effective running of a workshop with a co-leader requires those two leaders to be able to understand what each other's viewpoint is and to be able to back the other up where that is necessary. The ideal combination for a workshop on sexuality is to have one male and one female leader, especially when these two leaders are comfortable with each other's style and are well known to each other. This allows for a complementary viewpoint to be present with regard to issues of gender or where it may be felt by participants that because of the nature of the topic a person of one sex or the other is more appropriate to deal with a certain matter. When two people work together as co-leaders and their style is familiar, then they can act as an important source of support for each other throughout the day and afterwards providing feedback about each other's performance during the day. A single handed group leader does not have this level of support or feedback regarding his/her performance.

As previously stated, it is of course important to try to remain objective throughout the workshop, although it may be advantageous at times to adopt a role or position in order to facilitate discussion or provide a controversial viewpoint. This is something that must be gauged from the mood of the workshop and the level of functioning of the participants. The ability of the leaders to function effectively is soon gauged by the feedback obtained from the participants as the day progresses. As in all workshops or groups, there are times when a lot of energy needs to be involved in facilitating development of the process and group leaders must, therefore, be aware of the climate of the group as it progresses. Leaders must also be sensitive to issues that may be present as undercurrents of discomfort of workshop members which may not have been voiced or acknowledged. Although an outline is provided for the workshop it is important to establish that where issues become important, or a lot of discussion is taking place, the programme may need to be changed in order to accommodate what is important to the participants. On the other hand, it is of course important to avoid being side tracked unnecessarily with other issues.

It is important to realise that on running a workshop on sexuality, one's own sexuality may be questioned and direct personal questions asked. Although this is unlikely to happen, one must be prepared for this eventuality and if the subject matter is one that provokes discomfort, then leadership of the group should not be attempted.

Controversies

The subject of sexuality is one which inevitably is controversial. It is likely that nearly every area of sexuality has become controversial at some time and one has to remember that at the beginning of this century, matters such as masturbation were very controversial. Masturbation was thought by some to produce insanity and to be a very deviant form of sexual activity (Godfrey 1901). That controversy is probably generally resolved in that masturbation is no longer felt to lead to insanity, but in some areas it is still a controversial matter. In mental handicap the rights of an individual to masturbate or the teaching of masturbation where someone is unskilled at doing so, is a very controversial matter. This is an example of something that was seen to be controversial in the early part of this century and although it is resolved for part of the population, it is still controversial for other parts of the population.

In a workshop it is inevitable that controversial items will emerge and need to be discussed. The sort of things that will come up are sex roles and sexism, where norms and beliefs may vary throughout the country, but one may often find that acceptance is different from acknowledgement. Sex roles can be useful subjects for role-plays to explore this angle. Homosexuality is another area which is controversial particularly with the current hysterical reactions to AIDS in this country. (Although of course, AIDS is not restricted to homosexuals, it is homosexuals who are most identified with the disease). This is something else that can and should be raised at some time if appropriate during a workshop because of the large number of controversial statements and viewpoints that are current.

In relation to feminism and the exploitation of women the area of pornography will often be raised and this again is a controversial area. It can be viewed from the position that any pornography is degrading to women and therefore should not be available, or from another viewpoint, it is an extension of eroticism, erotic art and that its use can be very therapeutic in sexual therapy and also in some sex education.

Another item of controversy is the whole area of sex education and the delineation of responsibility for sex education. This has already been discussed earlier in the chapter, but is one item which does crop up consistently. With all of the aforementioned areas of controversy, it is important that opportunity is available to discuss these and that they can be fully aired in a non-judgemental way by the leader. It is inevitable that within the group of participants there will be differing views and all these should be heard. But remember that with a lot of these items the basic beliefs and ethical and moral values of individuals can be threatened and therefore sensitive handling of these is essential. It is extremely unlikely that any of these issues will be resolved within a workshop but their discussion is an important part of the process.

## Evaluation

It is important that any workshop that is undertaken can be evaluated at some stage. However, this produces problems of definition in that the efficacy of a given workshop may be not apparent at the time. It is important to try to obtain feedback at the end of the workshop via written forms or rating scales given to the participants and this can provide a fairly instant feedback of the success of various components of the workshop and of the general level of success. It is inevitable that different groups will present different sorts of feedback and for some groups this will be harder to obtain than from others.

However, one of the important aspects of evaluation is whether the workshop has made any significant changes over time and that the participants' time was worth spending in the workshop. This may not be something that is easy to obtain unless one has contact with the participants after the workshop and one has any measure of evaluation for the workshop. One way of doing this is to follow up to see what has been done in the area. For example, whether a sex education programme has been set up following a workshop or whether people are talking more about what they have done and whether in the long term people feel that they have a greater ability to talk about sexuality and whether this is relevant to their current working situation.

It is equally important for the workshop leaders to evaluate for themselves what they have achieved within that workshop, to look at possible areas of change, of development and success. Leaders need to be able to get together after a workshop to discuss these matters to ensure that what is learned from the day will be used on subsequent occasions. It is probably inevitable that each workshop run will produce some change in format, exercises adopted, changed or dropped, or style of presentation. Changes that have occurred include dropping exercises that prove too threatening, altering format to introduce an exercise at an earlier stage and most important- antly checking with participants whether they are present through choice or whether they have been 'sent' to the work- shop without being given the choice. This check was introduced after one workshop where some of the participants did not know why they were at the workshop or the nature of the content!

The ideas expressed in this chapter are by no means defin- itive and, as stated, are the result of experience. The model has been shown to be successful but is continually evolving and will do so as long as workshops are needed.

APPENDIX : SUGGESTED STATEMENTS FOR EXERCISE

It's alright for men to masturbate, but women shouldn't.
A man's sex drive is stronger than a woman's, so he needs to have sex more often.
It's not surprising so many women are raped, the way they dress they're just asking for it.
The age of consent for sex should be abandoned.
Most people find pornography a turn-on.
Women going to bed with each other is okay, but men going to bed with each other is disgusting.
It's not true that people sleep around a lot more now than they used to.
A man's looked up to if he sleeps around, a woman isn't.
Parents find it difficult to see their own children as sexual beings.
If a woman doesn't want to get pregnant, she should go on the pill.
You shouldn't go to bed with anyone unless you love them.
Catching V.D. nowadays is no problem.
Virginity is important.
If you're going out with someone you're expected to have sex with them.
Women have to cope with having periods each month, pregnancy and childbirth. Men have it easy!
Some people enjoy oral sex, some others say it's dirty and wrong. Who's right?

REFERENCES

Albery, N. (1984) 'Dice Therapy', Self and Society, 12(3),
    pp. 132-140
Atwell, B.M. (1984) 'Sex and the cancer patient: An unspoken
    concern', Patient Education and Counselling, Vol.5(3),
    pp. 123-126
Bell, S., Dickerson, M. and Stuckey, N. (1979) 'Human Sexuality
    in the Training of Clinical Psycholgists',Bulletin of the
    British Psychological Society, Vol. 32, pp. 68-70
Craft, A. and Craft, M. (1981) 'Sexuality and Mental Handicap:
    A Review', British Journal of Psychiatry, 139, pp. 494-505
Craft, A. and Craft, M. (1982) Sex and the Mentally
    Handicapped: A guide for parents and carers, Routledge
    and Kegan Paul, London
Dow, M.G.T. and Sclare, A.P. (1982) 'Teaching medical
    undergraduates about psychosexual problems', British
    Journal of Sexual Medicine, Vol. 8,(80) pp. 24-29
Fowles, J. (1969) The French Lieutenant's Woman, Jonathon Cape,
    London
Godfrey, J.A. (1901) The Science of Sex, The University Press,
    London
Kitzinger, S. (1982) 'Sexuality in Pregnancy', British Journal
    of Sexual Medicine, Vol. 9,(82) pp. 44-46
Nin, A. (1977) The Delta of Venus, W.H. Allen and Co., London
Parrot, A. (1984)'Sex Education Should Occur outside the Family
    in Schools, Youth Centres and Agencies',in Feldman, H. and
    Parrot, A. (eds), Human Sexuality, Contemporary
    Controversies, Sage Publications, London
Philliber, S.G. and Tatum, M.L. (1982) 'Sex education and the
    double standard in high school', Adolescence, Vol. 17(66)
    pp. 273-283
Sebba, J. (1981) 'Sexual Development in Mentally Handicapped
    People: A critical look at staff attitudes', APEX, Vol. 9
    No. 1, pp. 22-23
Steinbacker, J. (1984) 'Sex education is the right and
    responsibility only of the family', in Feldman, H. and
    Parrot, A. (eds), Human Sexuality, Contemporary
    Controversies, Sage Publications, London
Zwerner, J. (1982) 'Yes we have troubles but nobody is
    listening: sexual issues of women with spinal cord injury',
    Sexuality and Disability, Vol. 5(3), pp. 151-171

Chapter Eight

EVALUATING CHANGE AND DEVELOPMENT THROUGH WORKSHOPS

STEPHEN MURGATROYD

INTRODUCTION

At the end of a workshop the leader and the participants often
engage in evaluative conversations. These are usually formative: they are concerned with general impressions, are unspec-
ific and often concern the emotional tone of the experience. A
variety of adjectives are used in such conversations - challenging, interesting, demanding, moving, disquieting, evocative,
exhausting, instructive and surprising being amongst those
heard at the end of one of the workshops on stress described
earlier. Sometimes the leader may seek some more objective
evaluation of the outcome of the workshop - a more summative
evaluation. This may take the form of seeking to establish just
what changes in attitudes, behaviours or emotions have occurred
as a result of the workshop by means of interviewing, questionnaire, observation or some combination of these methods. In
addition, the leader may seek to examine the quality of the
workshop as a presentation so as to make changes to the format
in the light of experience - Rhys has made specific reference
to this in describing her health visitor workshops.

These forms of evaluation are the concerns of this concluding chapter. The aim is to examine the nature of changes that
can be expected from workshops and to understand the ways in
which such changes can be evaluated. The chapter is not intended to be a comprehensive introduction to evaluation methods
or to the technology of evaluation (but see Reason and Rowan
1981; Bogdan and Taylor 1975); rather, it is an attempt to
examine the issues which workshop leaders and participants
need to consider when seeking to engage in evaluation tasks.

It should be clear at the outset of this chapter that the
authors of this book feel strongly that workshops have a valuable place in the development of helping professionals - they
provide opportunities for exposure to processes and tasks which
are intended to directly affect the way helpers act, think and
feel. It should also be clear that the outcomes of the workshops described here are intended to be at a variety of levels.

For some workshops it is intended that they lead mainly to
direct changes in behaviour - that described by Hobbs is a
clear example of this. Others are intended to generally
encourage further reflection and insight - those described by
Shooter and Murgatroyd fall into this category. Yet others are
intended to provoke some careful thought about the management
and presentation of self whilst at the same time exploring
attitudes, behaviours, beliefs and values - the workshops
described by Pates, Woolfe and Rhys fall into this category. To
some extent, each workshop will be offering a combination of
these outcomes: they differ only in their intended emphasis.
Whilst these are the outcomes intended by the workshop leader,
participants may experience a great many other outcomes. These
can include (amongst others) the following: a feeling of
increased confidence, a strengthening of social support systems,
a new insight into an old experience, a fresh look at the process of learning or a new understanding of the skills needed to
achieve a particular goal. Given such a variety of levels of
'outcome' it is important to understand some of the dimensions
of learning that might be amenable to evaluation before examining the evaluation process.

SOME DIMENSIONS OF WORKSHOP LEARNING

In considering the outcomes of a workshop experience (or any
other learning experience for that matter) it is important to
have a clear understanding of the expectations that individuals
bring to that learning. In looking at why attitude and behavioural change do not occur as a result of workshops, it is
possible to use the findings of Baron (1968) and Kelman and
Baron (1968) to suggest that key features of such non-learning
are: 1. compartmentalisation - knowledge and experience have
become compartmentalised and the person expects a workshop to
maintain such compartmentalisation; 2. insulation - the person
has become separated from their actions in such a way that
learning about a subject (sex, death, stress, communication,
counselling) has become divorced from learning about self - any
workshop experience based upon linking self and subject becomes
threatening and the person uses denial, distortion, rationalisation or derogation of the workshop as a means of defending
their insulation; 3. ritualism - the person uses workshops to
bolster their status or their previously held views and rejects
experiences which challenge their status or views. These three
mechanisms of non-learning - compartmentalisation, insulation
and ritualism - are descriptions of three sets of expectations
(learning 'sets') which predispose participants to want certain
things from a workshop and to evaluate the workshop in terms of
its success in minimising the challenges to their 'self' and
skills.
     As an example of this 'non-learning', consider the case of
Sarah. She attended one of the stress workshops described

earlier in this volume. For her, all stress was caused by other people and she ritualistically blamed her parents for not helping her cope with people better. She saw all of her stress as resulting from things done to her - she was divorced from the way in which her own thoughts and actions contributed to her own stress. In this way, she insulated herself. Stress occurred for Sarah only at work (she said) and it did not affect her at home at all - she compartmentalised her experiences of stress. She was both rigid and dogmatic in expressing these views. The workshop leader had to work hard to encourage her to give herself permission to question these assumptions about herself and to learn.

The opposite of these three barriers to learning and change are more readily identifiable . Using some of the ideas developed by Rowan (1973) and derived from Fishbein (1967) and Rosenburg and Abelson (1958), those who expect to change and develop as a result of attending a workshop (albeit in a small but significant way) are those who: 1. link the process of learning and the content of a workshop to positive values; 2. attach as much importance to feelings and experience as they do to thoughts and actions; 3. are able to make linkages both between the subject matter of a workshop and the processes of that workshop and between their experience at the workshop and previous experiences; 4. feel able during a workshop or shortly thereafter to explore previously supressed values, beliefs or ideas; 5. are able to examine the ideas of others openly without undue defensiveness and with a view to integrating their ideas, thoughts and beliefs into their own thinking and experience; and 6. attend workshops because they see them as a means of opening themselves up to opportunities to learn rather than as being devices for confirming status and beliefs.

In describing these two sets of expectations and by describing them as unlearning and learning 'sets' it becomes clear that the way a participant approaches a workshop effects the outcome of the workshop for that person. Therefore, evaluation activities begin by exploring the different expectations that individuals have for the workshop that they are attending. This means that the process of evaluation begins as the ideas for the workshop are formulated: evaluation is not something simply completed at the end of the workshop but is an implicit feature of the workshop itself.

At several times in this collection of papers it has been noted that the organisers of workshops - those who contract our services - often make statements about the expectations of participants which are not then borne out by the statements made by the participants themselves. It has also been noted in several specific workshop descriptions (see especially those by Shooter, Pates and Rhys) that expectations about the kinds of learning from experience and reflection that can occur among the participants are varied.

In looking at the question of how expectations shape

159

outcomes, it is important to look also at how the leader of a
workshop looks at discrepancies and differences in expectations
amongst those with whom he or she is working and to look at the
use made of these differences throughout the workshop. A leader
who ignores the fact that different participants in a workshop
are seeking different outcomes may find that they are in conflict with one sub-group to such an extent that they are unable
to meet the expectations of any group within the workshop. A
leader who spends a considerable time negotiating and contracting with a group so as to overcome the process problems created
by radically different expectations can so eat away into the
time of the workshop that the subject matter of the workshop
gets diluted and its purposes lost. When looking at expectations it is therefore important to understand not simply what
they are but how they are used within the workshop to the
benefit of all participants.

LOCUS OF CONTROL

One dimension of learning which appears to tie strongly to
expectations can be referred to as 'locus of control'. This
refers to the extent to which a person feels that their thoughts
and actions are responses to environmental situations in which
others play a dominant role (external control) as opposed to
feeling that they are very much in control of their own envir-
onments and that their thoughts and actions, whilst showing
understanding of the views and actions of others, are very much
their own (internal control).
    The aim of all of the workshops described in this volume
is to increase the extent to which the person is able to
experience the world as something they themselves can shape and
control (internal control), though recognising that there are a
great many external forces and social conditions which make the
exercise of that control difficult. One way of thinking about
expectations is to think about the willingness of both participants and the leader to open themselves up to increasing the
extent of their internal control of experiences. It follows
from this that a task in evaluation is to explore the extent to
which a particular workshop has increased the feeling of
internal control amongst participants. Another way of describing the construct 'locus of control' is to think about workshops as aiming to increase the sense of personal autonomy
which participants experience during the workshop and can carry
from it (Hall, Woodhouse and Wooster 1984). This also relates
to the way in which participants show by their actions and
expression that they accept responsibility for their own
learning - a point explored fully in chapter one.
    Whilst there are some objective measures of locus of con-
trol which could be used to examine changes occurring between
the beginning and end of a workshop(see Lefcourt 1983; Hall
Woodhouse and Wooster 1984), many of the changes that we have

observed occur gradually rather than suddenly. Just as certain coping devices are summoned only when faced with a major stressor, so the experience of increased personal autonomy as a result of attending a stress workshop may only be apparent for some when a real and major stressor subsequently faces someone who was a participant at the stress workshops described by Woolfe and Murgatroyd. Measurements given as pre and post tests at a workshop may not, therefore, adequately reflect the extent of personally significant learning during that workshop (Collier 1977). In a formative evaluation, then, participants and leaders might usefully explore the extent to which this feature of learning has been experienced within the workshop.

## DEVELOPMENTAL VS IMMEDIATE LEARNING

Indicating that some of the benefits of a learning experience may not become apparent until that learning is called-out by some life event draws attention to another dimension of learning in workshops. It is that a great deal of the learning that leaders hope will accrue from their work (though not all) is developmental rather than immediate - is a 'dripping tap' kind of change rather than the opening of a floodgate. This means that changes that occur during or as a result of a workshop are not generally intended to be immediate and observable (though Hobbs does expect direct behavioural outcomes from his training work) but are intended to stimulate the person in their own development towards greater personal autonomy and a greater sense of their own internal locus of control.

## DEEP AND SURFACE LEARNING

At a minimum level, the changes which the workshops outlined in this volume are intended to encourage are related to increasing the participants' capacity for self-evaluation. This is achieved by encouraging self-disclosure, by active learning methods and by introducing new experiences (via role plays, games, simulations and direct teaching) and concepts. Enhanced self-evaluation coupled with increased awareness of the extent to which this can lead to better use being made of personal resources and relationships in a variety of settings leads to more opportunities for self-evaluation and for the exercise of personal autonomy. This 'deep level' learning - deep in the sense of its contribution to the ego development of the person and in terms of the kind of learning outcomes that it implies - underscores some of the surface learning outcomes that may be more readily observed - e.g. the use of a technical language to describe stress or bereavement or the use of a particular skill (dynamic meditation or systematic relaxation or assertiveness, for example).

Let us examine this idea of deep and surface learning a little further. It is possible for a person to be taught the

161

technical skills of writing - how to construct a paragraph,
how to structure an article.or a poem, how to make effective
use of adjectives when conveying feelings. These are surface
skills. For the person to show deep learning the person needs
to use these skills to reveal some insights about themselves or
others in their writing. That is to say, they express deeply
held views or beliefs and offer detailed observations in a way
that is a risk to them. In terms of the workshop on sexuality
described by Pates, some surface learning may occur about different sexual attitudes or behaviours. Deep learning would be
indicated by a person genuinely and honestly exploring their
own attitudes towards sexuality in a way that shows that they
are open to new learning and development.

In evaluating a workshop in terms of both its processes
and the outcomes it is important to understand that different
participants will experience different levels of learning at
the deep and surface levels and that not all of the learning
that has taken place can be discerned from a careful study of
the surface learning a person displays through their speech,
attitudes and behaviour.

INDIVIDUAL VS ORGANISATIONAL OUTCOME

A final dimension we consider important in the context of the
workshops we describe here concerns the extent to which outcomes are intended to be at the level of the individual (i.e.
relating to the individuals attending the workshop) and at the
level of the organisation of which that individual is a part.
For example, Murgatroyd describes a stress workshop which is in
part intended to assist individuals cope with the stress they
experience at work and in part to change those features of work
experience which many find stressful. In evaluating this workshop it is necessary to look at outcomes both in terms of the
individual participants and in terms of the organisational
consequences of the workshop. This also applies to some features
of several of the workshops described here. To provide another
example, Shooter describes death workshops which are intended
to encourage greater self-awareness and reflection on the
questions of death, dying, grief and bereavement. If this
workshop is offered to a specific group of nurses working in
a hospice it might be expected to lead to some change in the
practice of those nurses either in relation to grieving relatives or in relation to the grief nurses themselves experience
when a patient dies. In evaluating this workshop it may be
insightful to look at both the organisational as well as the
personal outcomes. These might include changes in rota arrangements, in the provision of rest room facilities or in the fre-
quency of staff meetings or some other organisational changes.

This review of certain key dimensions of the learning
experience in a workshop - expectations, locus of control, personal autonomy, developmental tasks and organisational change

- leads now to questions about how to evaluate both the process
and outcomes of workshops such as those described here.

EVALUATING LEADERSHIP

Hovland and his co-workers at Yale University (Hovland and Janis
1959; Hovland, Janis and Kelley 1953; Rosenberg and Hovland
1960) developed a programme of research which looked at the
kind of facilitator styles which were most likely to have an
impact on a group. They draw attention to the importance of
credibility in the success of a leader in a group or workshop.
They suggest that credibility consists of:-
1. The ability to communicate a sense of competence in
   relation to the topic which provides the focus for the
   workshop activity - this competence can derive either
   from scholarship or experience or some combination of
   both;
2. Being perceived as reliable as far as information
   sources are concerned - the extent to which workshop
   participants feel that the leader is dependable, pre-
   dictable and consistent;
3. Having one's motives clearly understood, especially in
   situations of conflict or when risks are being taken
   by participants;
4. Being empathic, warm and genuine in one's relations with
   participants;
5. The degree of dynamism or charisma displayed by the
   leader - indicated by the control and activity-
   leadership displayed and the extent to which participants feel confident about the direction offered by
   the leader; and
6. Majority opinion of the group - pressure towards con-
   formity in workshops is high.

The display and communication of such qualities permits the
leader to have a high level of influence upon the learning of
workshop participants.
   In some later development of this work, Janis (1982)
developed a detailed check-list of those features of helping
which maximised the helpers' ability to influence those with
whom they worked. Amongst the influencing skills which he
regards as critical are these:
1. Encouraging participants to make self-disclosures;
2. Giving positive feedback to participants and showing
   both acceptance and understanding of their feelings and
   thoughts;
3. Using helping skills to reshape thoughts presented by
   participants so as to encourage them to develop fresh
   insights;
4. Being concrete - making direct statements which endorse
   practical suggestions made by participants and which

give direction to some workshop or helping activity;

5. Eliciting commitment to taking some action (e.g. to read more, to discuss with a colleague some aspect of the workshop etc.) - encouraging participants to develop a self-contract for work as a result of the workshop process;

6. Showing that the ideas expressed by group members have antecedents in the work of other people - connecting 'naive' ideas to bodies of research and/or theory;

7. Giving selective positive feedback so as to shape the direction of an individual's development during a workshop;

8. Undertaking direct training of a person or sub-group or group so as to give some practical skills;

9. Giving reassurances to individuals within the group that they are learning and developing;

10. Being explicit about the contract for the workshop and its termination;

11. Giving reminders as to the major features of learning that have occurred during the workshop; and

12. Building up the confidence of participants that they can take some of the learning that has occurred during the workshop and apply it to situations which they encounter in the 'real' world.

These two lists of influencing skills are valuable when the workshop leader wishes to reflect on their own performance as a leader. They can be useful in exploring the style of leadership used and the extent to which any problems which emerged during the workshop can be related back to one or more of these features. Whilst not all of the items included in these two lists are relevant to all the workshops described in this volume, other workshops and other forms of training do involve these features.

These two lists are essentially concerned with three sets of leader characteristics. These are: 1. the disposition of the leader towards those who are to participate in the workshop - how he or she feels about the work they are to do and how he or she shows respect for the participants; 2. the attitudes that the leader encourages towards both the content of the workshop and the learning processes it involves and 3. specific behaviours of the leader. The lists given above (and others that you might construct for yourself) all relate to these three features of leadership.

There are, of course, some objective measures of leadership qualities which can be completed by participants so as to reveal to the leader how he or she is perceived. Some of the leadership check-lists given in Woodcock (1979), if adapted, can be useful for this purpose as also are those in Davis (1975).

Rhys, in her contribution to this book, stresses the importance of the leader being a learner both, during and after

the workshop they offer. This learning will take many forms,
and it is important for some of the work of leadership to
revolve around questions of influencing and supporting, since
this is the implicit purpose of many of the workshops described
here. All of the authors here give emphasis to the need for the
leader to be aware of their own 'self' and the way that this
'self' and its expression influences others.

EVALUATING THE WORKSHOP AS A PRESENTATION

A workshop is intended to be a form of learning experience in
which a leader seeks to facilitate the development of self-
disclosure, self-awareness, opportunity awareness, transition
learning and skill development. To do this he or she presents
a learning experience. One way of evaluating this experience
is in terms of the quality of the presentation.

Loughray and Hopson (1979) produce a very practical list
of items to examine when considering presentation. This
includes: 1. staff assignments - about the number of leaders,
the quality of administration of the workshop and about the
support personnel (e.g. catering, registration, secretarial
back-up, etc.); 2. media - about the availability of hardware
(e.g. video, audio replay, overhead and slide projectors, etc.)
and how operable this was once it became available; 3. participant concerns - ensuring that comments from participants about
rooms, meals, transportation or accommodation are borne in
mind when arranging a subsequent workshop; and 4. facilities -
were the coffee/tea, toilet and crèche arrangements satisfactory and was there a range of furniture suitable for those with
slight or serious disabilities? These sets of questions are
useful in looking at the administration of a workshop.

But questions of presentation go beyond these issues, as
Loughray and Hopson (1979) acknowledge. There is also a need
to ask some questions about goals: which were achieved  and
which were not?; how do you know that certain goals were
achieved - what is the basis for your assumption?; what are
the most useful outcomes of this workshop - does identifying
these change the goals you might have for the next workshop of
this kind? You might also want to examine the climate of the
workshop - list the adjectives you think are appropriate in
defining the climate of the workshop you have just completed:
on the basis of this list, what might you change the next time
you offer the workshop? Whilst not all of the workshops described here have such specific goals, some of these questions
may still be relevant.

Hall, Woodhouse and Wooster (1984) offer a detailed
evaluation of a workshop they offered to experienced teachers.
As a result of their evaluation, they conclude that 'it is
impossible to predict which event will be most potent for any
individuals'. This suggests that evaluation directed at presentation questions should examine the way the presentation

impacted on different participants: what are the individual
differences, were enough opportunities created during the
workshop to encourage individual learning, and how did you as
leader observe individual reactions and did you make adjust-
ments to the programme because of them? These questions (and
others you might generate) encourage reflection on the link
between the design of a workshop and its outcome.

Because adult learners bring a great many unique experiences with them into a workshop (Eraut 1982), the way in which
individuals are selected and grouped for workshops can be
important in shaping reactions to the presentation (Collier
1977). In thinking about presentation issues it is important
to ask questions about how participants were selected and what
this selection leads to in terms of the design of the workshop
- would it need to be different for different groups, what were
the effects of participants' status positions within their
profession upon their behaviour in the group, how did the
selection of participants affect the group's dynamics? These
questions help in planning subsequent workshops in which the
leader can influence participant selection and grouping.

EVALUATING OUTCOMES FOR PARTICIPANTS

When evaluation questions focus upon the direct outcomes for
participants in terms of attitudes, behaviours and feelings,
the evaluation task is much more difficult. Indeed, those who
offer workshops (both organisers and leaders) need to live
with a great deal of uncertainty about the benefits of their
work. This is because: 1. the intended outcomes from many of
the workshops described here are not amenable to direct observation or measurement; 2. some of the intended outcomes are
long term rather than short term; 3. many of the intended outcomes relate to attitudes rather than to behaviour, so they are
difficult to assess; and 4. the design of workshops seeks to
maximise individual learning, so there is a need to see outcomes
in terms of individual developments rather than in terms of the
group's development of skill. Each of these factors makes measurement of outcomes difficult and this, therefore, creates
difficulties about the way in which workshops can be evaluated.

Some attempts have been made to overcome these difficulties. There are several studies of the effects of workshops on
specific attitudes in which participants have been given attitude scales before, immediately after and some time after workshops so as to establish in some objective way the attitude
changes that take place. One example of this is a study by
Valerio and Stone (1982) of changes in attitudes as a result of
an assertiveness training programme. There are a number of
problems with such studies. The most significant problem is
that it is not easy to establish just what impact the workshop
itself has on attitude change over a long period (say 6-12
months) because a variety of things happen to a person during

this time which can also affect their attitudes. The second
major problem is that the measuring instruments used -
generally questionnaires - are not always designed to test for
changes in the specific attitudes or behaviours for which the
workshop is intended. Nonetheless, it is possible to show that
even brief learning experiences (6-10 hours) can have a significant impact on the attitudes of some participants.

Partly because of the technical difficulties and partly
because of the feeling which many workshop organisers and
leaders have that such objective evaluations become an intru-
sion into the workshop (see Hall, Woodhouse and Wooster 1984),
few workshops of the kind described here have been evaluated
in the way just described. More common are quasi-objective
evaluations. One exception to this general statement that
concerns the workshops described here are those developed by
Ivey (1971) and described above by Hobbs. These have been
evaluated in a variety of studies, most notably by Kasdorf and
Gustafsen (1978).

Quasi-objective evaluations take many forms. Rhys, in her
contribution, refers to letters which she asks participants to
write to themselves indicating what steps they are going to
take to continue their learning following the workshop (see
page 99 above). Such letters provide some materials from which
the leader is able to discern the kinds of experiences which
participants have found valuable. There are other such devices.
In some of the workshops on stress offered by Murgatroyd,
participants have written self-contracts about their own stress
management strategies for display in their offices: these
provide an indication of the skills which individuals have
attached importance to as a result of attending the workshop.
Others, such as Hall, Woodhouse and Wooster (1984) have asked
participants to participate in evaluative interviews shortly
after the workshop and these interviews have provided materials
which indicate the value of the workshops in terms of individual learning. Other devices that have been used in this way
include diaries completed before, during and after the workshops
- a comprehensive example of the value of this process for
evaluation is given in Ottaway (1966); video recording of
workshops which are then reviewed by participants (Breeze 1980;
Wright 1980) and various forms of self-report (Borodin 1968).

Workshop leaders should recognise the value of evaluative
statements made by participants during the course of a workshop. In some of the workshops described in this volume (notably
those offered by Woolfe, Rhys and Murgatroyd) participants are
asked to make evaluations at various points in the workshop and
to display these evaluations in the form of flip-chart comments
sheets. These sheets, if reflected upon after the workshop,
reveal many issues which are in the minds of participants at
various stages in the course of a workshop and can provide
valuable clues as to how to better structure either particular
activities or to the kinds of outcomes that can be expected to

arise as a result of the kinds of thoughts which such recorded statements reveal. In addition, they provide valuable materials which can be useful for participants at other subsequent workshops. To some extent, evaluation is an implicit feature of the workshop since almost all of the activities described in the earlier chapters contain evaluative components. The kind of questions asked and the responses of participants to specific workshop activities constitute evaluations.

If these approaches to evaluation appear 'soft' rather than 'hard' in terms of their data quality, this reflects the 'softness' of the workshop objectives. In many cases only generalised outcomes are intended; in such cases only generalised evaluations can take place. Only if learning objectives become explicit and specific can 'harder' and more objective evaluations be attempted.

CONCLUSION

As several writers on workshop evaluation have commented (see Loughray and Hopson 1979; Davis 1975 for example), it is better to undertake some evaluation activity than simply to assume that all is well. But the evaluations are likely to produce a variety of findings of different utility to the workshop leader. There are simply so many variables to be understood in the design and planning of a workshop and in determining outcomes that most evaluations are essentially formative rather than summative.

This observation leads to some comments about the nature of change that can be expected from a workshop. These comments are prompted by a review of our own evaluations of the workshops described in this book. First, the changes that some workshop participants report are not always obvious. For example, some of those who have attended the workshops described by Pates and Shooter indicate that the major outcome for them is an increase in their general social confidence - they feel more able to share their ideas in a group. In other cases, such as in the workshop described by Hobbs, the outcome for some has been increased awareness of the nature of communication in day to day life in addition to, generally, the development of particular communication skills. The development of increased confidence and awareness is not always something that is easy to observe.

A related point is that change is not always neat and tidy. A change in attitudes towards death or the development of a new skill in stress management may have effects on other aspects of a person's life that take time to 'sort out'. For example, one woman discovered her need to develop her assertiveness skills on a stress management course offered by Woolfe which led her to seek further support because of the impact her assertiveness was having upon her husband. A change in one aspect of this person's life had consequences in another.

A third feature of change processes is that change is not
always transferable. Murgatroyd (1986), looking at social
skills training programmes, observes that it is not always
possible to transfer skills learnt in workshops into social
situations. Indeed, a classical problem with all forms of
training is the extent to which training is transferable from
one setting to another - an issue examined extensively by
Pribram (1964). If workshop leaders intend their participants
to develop skills which are transferable to the social world
or to a variety of planned situations, then the evaluation of
these skills ought to reflect this assumption.

One final point about change. Change is not always permanent. Law (1977) observes that teachers on in-service training
may develop new skills and attitudes during an intensive or
long training programme which then are modified during their
period of readjustment to the school of college. Indeed, in his
study of the impact of counsellor education he shows that
teachers who trained as counsellors soon return to their former
belief and value positions when working in schools, despite an
initial change in these attitudes and values on leaving training (Law 1978). If workshops are intended to have both short
and long term consequences for participants then the process of
evaluation ought to reflect this assumption.

In a chapter of this length it is not possible to examine
all aspects of evaluation. The reader has already been referred
to two sources of detailed comments about evaluation processes
(see Reason and Rowan 1981; Bogdan and Taylor 1975). There is
an excellent text devoted to assessment by Derek Rowntree (1977)
which ends with the suggestion that all assessments of students
should end with a government health warning: 'relying too
heavily on other people's opinions can damage your sense of
reality' (p.243). In the context of workshop evaluations, this
text might be amended to read: 'relying too heavily on measures
of outcome can damage the quality of a workshop's progress and
the value, extent and future impact of participants' learning'.
For there is a danger in workshop evaluation that the quality
of the learning experiences will be neglected in the pursuit of
a larger number of discernable and permanent outcomes.

## REFERENCES

Abelson, R.P. and Rosenberg, M.J. (1958) 'Symbolic Psycho-Logic
- A Model of Attitudinal Cognition', Behavioural Science,
Vol. 3 , pp. 16-21
Baron, R.M. (1968) 'Attitude Change through Discrepant Action
- A Functional Analysis', in Greenwald, A.G., Broch, T.C.
and Ostrom, T.M. (eds), Psychological Foundations of
Attitudes, Academic Press, New York
Bogdan, R. and Taylor, S.J. (1975) Introduction to Qualitative
Research Methods - A Phenomenological Approach to the
Social Sciences, John Wiley and Sons, New York

Bordin, E.S. (1968) Psychological Counselling (2nd Edition), Appleton-Century Crofts, New York

Breeze, J. (1980) 'The Use of Video Recordings in the Training of Counsellors', New Era, Vol. 61(5), pp. 196-198

Collier, J. (1977) 'Research in Small Group Methods in In-Service Work', British Journal of In-Service Education, Vol. 4(1), pp. 74-77

Davis, L.N. (1975) Planning Conducting and Evaluating Workshops, Learning Concepts, Auston, Texas

Eraut, M. (1982) 'What is Learned in In-Service Education and How? A Knowledge Use Perspective', British Journal of In-Service Education, Vol. 9(1), pp. 6-13

Fishbein, M. (1967) Readings in Attitude Theory and Measurement, John Wiley and Sons, New York

Hall, E., Woodhouse, D.A. and Wooster, A.D. (1984) 'An Evaluation of In-Service Courses in Human Relations', British Journal of In-Service Education, Vol. 11(1), pp. 55-60

Hovland, F. and Janis, I. (1959) Personality and Persuadability, Yale University Press, New Haven

Hovland, C., Janis, I. and Kelley, H. (1953) Communications and Persuasion, Yale University Press, New Haven

Ivey, A. (1971) Microcounselling: Innovations in Interview Training, Thomas, Springfield, Illinois

Janis, I. (1982) 'Helping Relationships - A Preliminary Theoretical Analysis', In Janis, I. (ed), Counselling on Personal Decisions, Yale University Press, New Haven

Kasdorf, J. and Gustafsen, K. (1978) 'Research Related to Micro-Training', in Ivey, A. and Authier, J. (eds) Microcounselling - Innovations in Interviewing, Counselling, Psychotherapy and Psychoeducation, Thomas, Springfield, Illinois

Kelman, H.C. and Baron, R.M. (1968) 'Determinants of Models of Resolving Inconsistency Dilemmas: A Functional Analysis', in Abelson, R.P. et. al. (eds), Theories of Cognitive Consistency - A Sourcebook, Rand McNally, New York

Law, W.M. (1977) 'What Do Teachers Learn from In-Service Guidance Training?, The Counsellor, Vol. 2(2), pp. 8-30

Law, W.M. (1978) 'The Concomitants of System Orientation in Secondary School Counsellors', British Journal of Guidance and Counselling, Vol. 6(2), pp. 161-175

Lefcourt, H. (ed), Research Using the Locus of Control Concept, Academic Press, New York

Loughray, J.W. and Hopson, B. (1979) Producing Workshops, Seminars and Short Courses - A Trainer's Handbook, Cambridge, New York

Murgatroyd, S. (1985) Counselling and Helping, British Psychological Society/Methuen, London

Pribram, K.H. (1964) 'Neurological Notes on the Art of Education', in Hilgard, E.R. (ed), Theories of Learning and Instruction, University of Chicago Press, Chicago

Reason, P. and Rowan, J. (1981) Human Inquiry - A Sourcebook of New Paradigm Research, John Wiley, London

Rosenberg, M. and Hovland, C. (eds) (1960) Attitude, Organization and Change, Yale University Press, New Haven

Rowan, J. (1973) Psychological Aspects of Society - The Science of You, Davis Poynter, London

Rowntree, D. (1977) Assessing Students - How Shall We Know Them?, Harper and Row, London

Valerio, H.P. and Stone, G.L. (1982) 'Effects of Behavioural, Cognitive and Combined Treatments for Assertion as a Function of Differential Deficits', Journal of Counselling Psychology, Vol. 29(2), pp. 158-168

Woodcock, M. (1979) Team Development Manual, Gower Press, London

Wright, P. (1980) 'The Use of Video Tape Recordings in the Training of Counsellors', New Era, Vol. 6(5), pp. 191-195

INDEX

Abelson, R.P. 159
adolescents 144, 151
Alberti, R.E. 34
Albery, N. 140
Andrews, L. 113
anticipatory coping 28
Apter, M.J. 23
Argyle, M. 89
Argyris, C. 41
Aries, P. 114
arousal 22-3
assertiveness 33-5
Attwell, B.M. 141
Authier, J. 64

Balfour-Sclare, A. 127
Bandler, R. 52
Baron, R.M. 158
Barton, D. 120
Beck, A.T. 29
Beckhard, R. 42
Beehr, T.A. 41
Bell, D. 91
Bell, S. 136
Bennis, W.G. 42
bereavement see death
Berenson, B.G. 85
Berne, E. 8
Bertman, S.L. 119
body language 69-70
Bogdan, R. 157, 169
Bond, M. 24
Borodin, E.S. 167
brainstorming 22, 49-50
Brandes, D. 46, 57
Breeze, J. 167

Bridge, W. 90
buffer strategy 28-9

Caplan, G. 16
Carkhuff, R.R. 85
change 168-9
    evaluation of see evaluation
    organisational 54-7
Chernis, C. 40
Clark, J.M. 90
cognitive restructuring 29-31,
    33
Collier, J. 161, 166
communication 89-91
    non-verbal 69-70
    training in 61-79
    attentive listening 67-72
    integration of skills 78-9
    micro-counselling 64-5
    paraphrasing 75-7
    questions 72-5
    reflection of feelings 77-8
    skills 62-4, 169
contracts 10-12, 50
control, locus of 160-1
Cooper, C.L. 40
counselling 61-79, 112
Craft, A. and M. 137
Crase, D.C. 113
Crase, D.R. 113, 133
crisis-management strategy 29

Davis, L.N. 164, 168
Davis, M. 30
death: helping the dying and
    bereaved 111-33

Index

# Index